FOUR PAWS
and 31 TALES

Stories to benefit
Four Paws Lifeline

Four Paws and 31 Tales

Copyright © 2016
FourPawsLifeline.org

Copyrighted stories were donated by the following authors:

Barbara Strunin	Lillian Spiro
Brenda Sandeland	Linda Rettstatt
Callie Machan	Linda Schmidt
Carolyn Cullen	Lisa Reed
Carolyn Prentkowski	Mary Roever
Dana Moody	Michelle Rueda
Deborah Courville	Sass MacConney
Debs Spencer	Shannon Glarium
Elizabeth Culver	Sharon Fletcher
Gator's mom, Laura	Shauna Gibb
Heidi O'Connor	Shayna O'Connor
Janice Robinson	Tami Schipper
Jennifer Niemi	Terry Cramer
Kathy Hudak	Verna Gibb
Kimberley Koz	Victoria Jane Townsend

The cover models are TSK Moody and Daffy Trinka-Moody, beloved furkids who live with Dana and Jim Moody.

ISBN-10: 1533514593
ISBN-13: 978-1533514592

DORA'S STORY
AND HOW FOUR PAWS LIFELINE CAME TO BE

I began thinking about this project in October 2013 after my cat JC had his leg removed, and was ultimately diagnosed with cancer. But I had real doubts that I could pull it off. I was just an animal lover who had their best interest at the forefront of my mind.

Then in October 2014 the concept came rushing back when Dora, my newest rescue, swallowed a small piece of rubber and had to have emergency surgery. I was able to take care of this large vet bill with Carecredit. But it occurred to me that there are those that would have had to have their pets euthanized because they wouldn't have been able to afford this.

Once again I thought about what I could do. I started talking to people and got very encouraging responses. I mentioned it to a couple of my Twitter friends and they quickly volunteered to help. So, I started the process to find out what I needed to do to start a non-profit organization. I took it one step at a time, and with the amazing help of Dana and Kim, I have my online presence.

My hope is that we are able to raise funds to help pets like Dora who find themselves in emergency situations to live a long and happy life. I hope that you will help us!

Karen Brothers
Founder and Director
Four Paws Lifeline

A 501(c)(3) non-profit organization
Tax ID #47-2991797

www.FourPawsLifeline.org
#217
8825 34th Ave NE, Suite L
Tulalip, WA 98271-8086

guardian@FourPawsLifeline.org
Fax: 360-558-7950

TABLE OF CONTENTS

ACKNOWLEDGMENTS

Thank you to the following authors who donated their story to this project. Profits from the sale of this book benefits
Four Paws Lifeline.

Barbara Strunin

Brenda Sandeland

Callie Machan

Carolyn Cullen

Carolyn Prentkowski

Dana Moody

Debs Spencer

Deborah Courville

Elizabeth Culver

Gator's mom, Laura

Heidi O'Connor

Janice Robinson

Jennifer Niemi

Kathy Hudak

Kimberley Koz

Lillian Spiro

Linda Rettstatt

Linda Schmidt

Lisa Reed

Mary Roever

Michelle Rueda

Sass MacConney

Shannon Glarium

Sharon Fletcher

Shauna Gibb

Shayna O'Connor

Tami Schipper

Terry Cramer

Verna Gibb

Victoria Jane Townsend

ONCE UPON A TIME...

Herman, a red and white Turkish Angora, watched his little sister, a petite tabby, playing with her pink catnip mouse. "Time for bed, Dori."

"Already? But I'm not sleepy."

"Mom told me to put you to bed. Now. Let's go."

Dori picked up her mouse. "Mom said I was a good girl today." She followed him through the house to her room. "I didn't break anything."

Herman's whiskers twitched with humor. "That's always a plus. Do you need a drink of water, or to go potty before you go to sleep?"

"I'm good." She climbed into her flowery pink bed. As Herman tucked a blanket around her she said, "Don't you think I deserve a reward for not breaking anything today?"

"Mom said no more bedtime treats. They promote tooth decay."

"Not treats...although I think that rule is unfair. I may sue to get my Smittens back. No, I think you should read me a story."

Herman reached for a thin book of one minute bedtime stories.

"Not that one." Dori pulled a larger book out from under her pillow. "This one."

Herman read the title. "*Four Paws and 31 Tales.* Dori, this

1

could take all night to read."

Her bright eyes watered with disappointment. "But Hwermie, I was a good girl today. Please. Please read this book to me."

Herman glanced at the clock, then sighed. He had intended to call his best girl, Belle, and meow sweet nothings into her ear, but... Dori hadn't broken anything that day, and that was rare enough to warrant a reward.

"Okay. I'll read to you. But the moment you fall asleep..."

"I'm not tired," Dori insisted. She fluffed her pillow, and snuggled with her pink mouse. "You know what would make this even more Wonderpurr? A bag of Smittens."

Herman hid his smile behind the book. "Chapter One..."

TSK: TIME SHARE KITTY

My life began in Southern California where I was born a petite brown tabby with a white muzzle. I was called Starsky and my brother was called Hutch after the TV show that ran in the mid-seventies. We had a nice life with our person, an elderly lady. But then Hutch passed away and my person got ill and wasn't able to care for me. She had to go into an assisted living place that didn't allow cats. How rude! However, the lady had a friend whose daughter was an animal lover and offered to take me, but she lived eight hours away in the mountains. Good thing I like car rides.

So off I went to live in the mountains...with a BIG dog. And two rambunctious boys. And snow. I don't like snow. Or the cold. Where was my sunny SoCal weather? Where was my quiet home? And my sweet elderly person? I spent a good portion of the time in my new home under the bed. I don't mind dogs, but those boys were too much for me.

Then, one day while I was outside, I met a nice couple who lived across the way. They let me come into their home to enjoy some peace and quiet. They called themselves Jim and Dana. And happily, they now belong to me.

You see, for many months they only came to the mountains on the weekends. I always sensed when they would be coming and I would wait on their porch. "Hurry up," I would meow. We would have lots of fun on the weekends, but then came Sunday afternoon and they would take me back to the house with the noisy kids. I couldn't wait until the next Friday for Jim and Dana to return.

Sometimes I would be so excited to see them, I would leave little tokens of appreciation on their porch.

They called me Time Share Kitty. T.S.K. for short. Some people mistakenly refer to me as 'tsk.' That's not my name. I'd ever do anything that would warrant someone saying "tsk tsk" to me.

Then, one wondrous day, Jim and Dana moved to the mountains full time. And the noisy boys' mother agreed I should live with them. Not only on the weekends, but every day. I was so happy!

It's been great having Jim and Dana as my forever staff. They take me places in the motorhome they bought just for me. I'm an excellent traveler. And I will walk on a leash and harness (as long as you walk where I want to go).

One day they sat me down and told me we were moving to Oregon, and that they would find me the best house to live in. I was cool with that. So we packed my beds and blankies, and off we went in my motorhome. They did find the best house for me, but sadly we had to wait for it to be ready for us to move into. We lived in my motorhome for three whole months. It wasn't bad at first since it was nice weather and I got to go outside and hang out in my KritterKondo. But then it started getting cold. There is heat in my motorhome, but I like things toasty so I had them build me a little tent over the heater vent. My staff is awesome.

When the day finally arrived for us to move into our new home, I was so happy. I ran from room to room, tail held high, checking everything out. There are stairs to play on and lots of windows for Cat TV and sun puddles. *Ahhhhh, this is the life!* I thought. But that isn't the best part.

A couple of years ago my staff brought home a dog. I could tell Daffy was a very special dog, so I welcomed her with a nose tap to let her know that I would be her big brother and help her settle in. She was very appreciative, and now we are great pals.

I've been thinking, as I'm no longer a Time Share Kitty, I should change what T.S.K. stands for. Maybe… The Sweetest Kitty. Or The Smartest Kitty. Hm. Perhaps it doesn't matter what I'm called.

As long as Jim and Dana love me, I have a Happily Ever After kind of life, and that's what's really important.

TSK's story is donated by Dana Moody @DanaPixie.

DAFFODIL: THE BLOOMING DOG

My name is Daffy, short for Daffodil. You see, my mom named me that with hope that I would blossom. And blossom I did! Let me tell you how I did that.

You see, the first few years of my life weren't very happy. I lived with a farmer who cared enough to get me fixed and have my needle jabs, but then one day... I don't know what I did wrong, but I was tossed outside to fend for myself. I had no place else to go, so I stayed there on the farm. I had no shelter or food. I had to scrabble with the chickens for their food. I was cold in snowstorms and I was scared. I no longer trusted people. One day a rescuer found me and brought me to the shelter.

Meanwhile, my future mom had been without a dog for two years since her beloved long-haired Dachshund, Betsy Ross, had made her journey over the Rainbow Bridge. She prayed that somehow a dog would come to her that would be just the right fit for her, and her for the dog. A woman at the place mom worked told her she had just rescued a dog and showed her my photo.

My future mom said no. She wanted luxurious fur and big brown eyes. I was a mess. I had an ulcerated stomach and I had stinky breath because my teeth were bad. I couldn't give kisses even if I wanted to, so I stayed at the shelter.

Eight months later a friend of my future mom's said she had a dog she didn't want anymore. That dog was me, but Mom didn't know that at the time. When she came over to meet me, I growled at her. I didn't mean to, it just came out because I was scared.

When Mom said she didn't want me, the lady told her my story, and it finally dawned on Mom that I was the same dog that her coworker had told her about. She felt that this was a sign. She was being given a second chance to have me. And so she took me home and changed my name to Daffodil. She told me I was going to 'blossom' there with her.

I wasn't the best girl though. I was afraid of people and everything. I would cower under the table or hide in my crate and not want to come out. I wouldn't make eye contact with anyone. But Mom was very patient with me, and after a year of working with me I did blossom. She taught me tricks. I was a quick learner. She said I was smart!

Sometimes Mom was unable to take me for walks and would ask a Boy Scout to do it. In winter the Scout would shovel a path for me to go potty since I don't like the snow. After some time passed I realized my mom was sick, and getting more and more sick. I became her nurse, sitting with her when she felt bad, walking behind her when she was unstable on her feet, keeping a watchful eye out in case she stumbled. I slept next to her in the big bed, and every night she told me she loved me. She had saved me and wanted only the best for me.

As time went on I could tell she was feeling worse and worse, and it made me anxious. Mom told me a day would come when she would no longer be able to care for me. That made me really sad, but then she said she had made arrangements with one of my pals on Twitter (I had a lot of pals there) and that I would go live with them. She reassured they would love me as much as she loved me, though I didn't think that was possible.

Suddenly, my life went back to being scary. Mom went in and out of the hospital many times. I had to stay in a kennel at the vet's office. I didn't like that. I was nervous and scared, and I missed my mom. One of mom's few friends took me to her house. That was better, but I still wanted to be home with my mom.

Then one day... I knew. The day Mom had prepared me for had come. I felt her in my heart, telling me that she had gone to heaven. She asked me to be a good girl for the people that would become my new forever family, and I promised I would.

Soon after, strangers arrived to pack up my food and toys and sweaters. And me! I heard Mom telling me not to be afraid. I was about to start a new life.

I was driven 1500 miles across 5 states in 3 days by nice people who turned out to be my dear friends on Twitter. Everyone was so kind and caring, and I am forever grateful to them for getting me to my new home. If I wasn't so confused about what was happening, I would have been in awe that thousands of people were following my journey on Twitter. Even someone in Australia stayed up all night to make sure I got to my new home. Wow!

Then I met my new people: Ms Pixie and Mr Pixie. My mom and I had chatted with them a lot over the years, so I knew right then that everything was going to be okay.

On the drive to Oregon to what would become my new forever home, they told me about all the things that we would be able to do, and that I was going to have a brother. I had never had any siblings and I was unsure around other animals, but the Pixie's told me not to worry. They would help me adjust to my new life. And when we finally arrived at my new home—guess who met me at the door? My new brother, TSK! He even gave me a nose tap to welcome me.

The very next day a reporter and photographer from the local paper interviewed me. I was going to be famous! Mom never said anything about that, though I kept hearing her voice in my heart, telling me to be a good girl, to just be myself. I also heard her say she would always watch over me from heaven, and she would love me forever. It made me sad that I would never feel her gentle hand upon my head, or that I wouldn't be able to do the tricks for her that she taught me. But I was excited to show the Pixie's all the great things that my mom taught me to do, and they agreed that I would be a wonderful part of their family.

So now I have lived with the Pixie's for two years, and I am proud to say that I have had two blossomings! I blossomed for my mom, and was the best dog that she needed me to be: a nurse and a companion to her. And then I blossomed for a second time with the Pixie's, as I am learning to be just a dog and do dog stuff that I had never dreamed of doing.

Since I moved in with the Pixie's I took agility lessons and ran the agility course. I became a Canine Good Citizen. I learned to be a great trail dog and hiker, and I have gone skiing (ok, I had booties on while the Pixie's skied). I have even gone 'Stand Up Paddling.' Me! The dog who was afraid of everything. Can you believe that? I have some dog pals, too: Scruffy lives next door and Mariner lives across the court. And guess what? TSK and I are great pals! We run and play. He likes to groom me, too. I don't quite get why he does that, but I let him anyway.

So that is my story. I blossomed, just like my mom said I would. I miss her every day, but I know she is happy and proud of me. She will forever be in my heart. She will always be a part of me.

Daffy's story is donated by Dana Moody @DanaPixie

THE MEOW GIRLS

Penny & Tippy, better known as the Meow_Girls on Twitter, are crazy for Temptations Cat Treats. Anytime someone walks past their treat bowls, they stand at attention at their respective bowls and yowl. Don't try to ignore them because they will not *stop*.

One morning my sister Annie and I decided not to give in to their pitiful meows, and ignored their begging.

Suddenly, I heard a crash. I turned to see Penny on the kitchen counter with Tippy below her, inspecting their open treat jar that had scattered their tasty treasures across the floor. Mission accomplished, Penny joined Tippy to enjoy their pirated plunder.

Needless to say, we learned a lesson: When the Meow_Girls want treats, they get them. Not too many. Just enough to stop the floor show.

The @Meow_Girls story is donated by Kathy Hudak.

THE CAT WHO CAME TO STAY

I once remarked to a neighbour that I'd never owned a cat. "Of course you haven't," she replied witheringly. "You don't own cats. They own you."

At the time I didn't believe her. Some people have to learn everything the hard way.

It was late one night when I heard the plaintive meowing in the garden. As I opened the door the light from the hall-way was reflected back from a pair of amber eyes.

Making pitiful little "feed me" sounds, the cat sidled up to me and rubbed himself ingratiatingly against my legs.

He was a beautiful animal. His body was as amber as his eyes, except for his white paws and distinctive white rings around his tail. He looked up at me with a wheedling expression and meowed imploringly.

I'd always been nervous of cats, but I couldn't resist tickling behind his ears. He purred his pleasure. I was hooked.

The dog would have had something to say about it if I'd taken him in, of course, but it was a mild night. I put out a saucer of milk and closed the door.

Ten minutes later I opened it again to find the cat sitting hopefully on the doorstep. The saucer was licked clean. I refilled it and added a few chunks of the dog's uneaten dinner. He wolfed it.

Opening the door again half an hour later I was disappointed to see no sign of him...till I looked across the garden. There he lay, curled up in a blissful sleep under the lilac tree, beside a baby hedgehog.

In the morning he'd gone but he returned at tea-time, meowing confidently, and was fed. He tried to push past me into the house but, hearing the dog's undisguised fury as he hurled himself at the kitchen door, thought better of it.

The following afternoon the weather turned nasty. A torrential downpour had lasted all morning, and the meowing on the doorstep put me in a quandary.

I couldn't possibly take him in. I didn't know anything about looking after cats, and the dog would probably have him for breakfast—or vice versa.

On the other hand I couldn't very well leave him out in the storm.

Shutting the dog in the kitchen, I opened the door.

The shivering bundle of soggy fur that looked piteously up at me would have melted a heart of permafrost. On impulse I picked him up and, ignoring the dog's howls of protest, installed him in the guest room.

By tea-time the newcomer had his own litter-tray, food and dishes, biscuits, blankets and some mouse-like toys. The only problem was making sure the cat and dog never came face to face. I became quite skillful at letting the dog into the back garden and the cat into the front, taking care not to let their paths cross.

The cat was happy under the bed in the guest room, so the dog could have the run of the rest of the house as usual. Everything was going fine. Then disaster struck.

Once the dog stopped growling threateningly from outside the guest room door I decided that the time had come to introduce them. With hindsight, this was not the wisest thing I've ever done. I can only say that it seemed like a good idea at the time.

Cat and dog faced each other across the kitchen floor. Neither uttered a sound. The atmosphere was electric. I suddenly I realized I was holding my breath, and forced myself to let it out again.

They were staring at each other like two Western gunslingers, but so far neither had attacked. Hope was beginning to stir. It was going to be all right.

It wasn't.

The dog moved a paw, and the cat lashed out. The dog wasn't standing for that and took off, baying.

As I snatched the cat out of harm's way he spat viciously at the dog, and sank his claws deep into my arm for good measure. I howled louder than the dog.

The dog made a determined lunge at the cat's long, elegant tail, trailing temptingly underneath my arm. I swung round to prevent contact. The dog's teeth missed the cat's tail by a hairsbreadth and embedded themselves firmly in my own rear end, instead.

I howled louder than a whole pack of dogs. The cat was returned forcibly to the guest room while I went in search of antiseptic and a large, consoling whiskey.

A few days later, as suddenly as he'd arrived, the cat disappeared. Dinner-time came and went. Bed-time did the same.

Convinced he'd been run over, I wrapped up his blanket and put his toys away. The dog, allowed back into the guest room, sniffed in bewilderment under the bed and then took up guard duty outside the door. The house was very quiet.

A week later I passed the local hairdresser's, glanced absent-mindedly at the cat sunning itself on the door-step, and did a double-take. The car screeched to a halt, and I ran back down the road to take a look.

I'd have known those amber eyes, white paws and white-ringed tail anywhere, but if it was mutual he wasn't letting on. He allowed me to tickle him behind his ears, but without the slightest sign of recognition.

The hairdresser opened the door and the cat stood up, stretched himself and stalked haughtily past her into the shop.

"I was wondering where he'd got to," she said cheerfully. "He's dreadful for wandering. He sometimes doesn't come back for a fortnight at a time. They're such a worry, aren't they?"

"They certainly are," I agreed fervently, and headed back towards the car.

So the pathetic little waif had a perfectly good home all along and had just fancied a change of scene!

I was furious with myself for being taken in.

Cats? You can keep them.

Dinner was over and I'd settled down to watch TV when something alerted the dog. Going to the front door he listened carefully for a moment, then began baying in a now-familiar way. I shut him in the kitchen and opened the front door.

It was raining heavily, and there on the doorstep stood a bedraggled little kitten. I knew her by sight. She had belonged to an elderly neighbour who had recently died.

I told myself firmly that I'd had enough of cats. They're condescending creatures that wrap themselves around your heart-strings, get you bitten by the dog, and then disown you.

The kitten meowed piteously, wound herself around my ankles and looked longingly past me into the house.

Behind the kitchen door the dog was yelping in joyous anticipation of battles to come. Rain trickled like tears off the kitten's whiskers as she looked up into my face.

Well, there were several tins of cat-food still unopened in the kitchen. It would be a shame to waste them.

The kitten purred her gratitude as I picked her up. Making a mental note to stock up on antiseptic and sticking plasters, I took her in and closed the door.

Shayna O'Connor ~ @ShaynaCat ~ has donated this story to benefit Four Paws Lifeline.

LINNY

My story starts out with my new beginning. My name is Linda, but I'm called Linny, and as I write this I am happy to tell you I've been in my forever home for nearly one year.

See, last winter I found myself outside in back-to-back snow storms. I was freezing and starving. I meowed at so many people passing by to help me that I was losing my voice, but no one stopped to even ask, "What's wrong?" They ignored me as if I didn't exist. But I did exist! I was a rare orange female tabby, and that made me special. But getting busy people to notice me was so very hard.

Then I heard about a place where humans feed street cats. I could hardly walk, I was so cold and hungry, but I managed to find that place. And yes, there was food and yes, I got fed. What I didn't know was, after I'd eaten, that I'd be scooped up in a sweater and made warm. It felt so good to be warm, and have a full tummy. But most of all, it felt wonderful to be held, to feel as though someone really cared about me. But what would happen after I warmed up? Would I be sent back out into the freezing cold, not knowing when I'd eat again?

But I wasn't. Instead I was taken to a No Kill Shelter where I stayed for a few weeks to get round-the-clock care. They said I was malnourished, and I had nearly frozen to death. I was scared, but the nice people gave me plenty of food and water and blankets.

That spring I went to live in my new forever home. I have a grade IV heart murmur and can't get spayed unless I get tests done, but I'm happy now. I have six brothers and one sister to play with, and I have a title: 'Room Monitor' because if my fursibs quarrel over cat nip and toys, I step in to keep the peace. I don't want anyone ruining my contentment and bliss. At last I've found my purrrfect Forever Home!

Linny's story is donated by Lillian Spiro. @SpookyShorty

SADIE GETS IN LINE

Woof! I am Sadie, a four-year-old American Eskimo and Pomeranian mixed breed. Raised in Colorado, I have captured the hearts of my two humans. They are my parents. Before they came along, I was raised alone and thought I liked to be alone, but nope. I was wrong. In fact, I love a good gang. A gathering.

A gaggle you might say.

One day while out on my trail walk, which I take rain or shine, I spied a family of ducks waddling single-file in front of me.

Oooo, I thought. *What are these fun creatures? Why are they walking in such a funny formation? How many can I play with and when do I start?* I pounced merrily to catch up to this group, but was told by my daddy to behave.

Pfft, I thought. *I am behaving.* So I slow-walked him into formation behind me and tried to catch up with the single-file fun. When the momma duck picked up the pace, I did too. I could hear my daddy mumbling under his breath, but also heard him giggling.

As we—ducks, dog and human—happily walked in line, we passed the lake where turtles sunned themselves on a rock. I said to one of the turtles, *Look at me. I have joined a ducky walking line.* When the turtle nodded his approval, I wagged my tail.

Suddenly I noticed the last of the four ducklings had fallen back from the hustling gaggle of fowl fun. I thought, *Oh this one wants to be friends.* But when I sped up to say hello to the little ducky, its momma and the other ducklings hit the gas. As they quickly waddled ahead, the last little duck seemed to walk even slower.

Seeing this was my chance, I flashed my soulful puppy eyes on my daddy and, being the soft, easy-touch-of-a-guy he is, he allowed me get pretty close to the straggling duckling. So close that I actually sniffed him! He waved his tiny tail feather at me, and though he slowly waddled after his momma, he kept looking at me over his shoulder. Me! His new friend!

I told him, *My name is Sadie. Do you want to be pals?*

I watched as he picked up one webbed foot and then another, and shook them in turn at me. Maybe this was his way of saying 'Yes,' he wanted to pals. *This is the best*, I thought. *I have got to master that foot move with my own paws.*

I looked at my paws. No webs, but still fun to shake shake shake. I made my collar rattle, shook out my fur and got back in line behind my new tiny fuzzy ducky pal, making sniffing noises and wagging my tail ever so gently so as not to scare him.

Eventually the baby duckling was told by his momma to stop dawdling and catch up. I followed suit, but knew it was time for us both to go home.

As we walked along, I thought we made quite a parade: Momma duck first in line, three fuzzy baby ducklings, a long space—then my new fuzzy ducky pal—then me and my daddy. I could fancy myself a member of this fun duck family. I even waddled slightly with my leash fully extended.

When I'm out on my daily walks, I usually chase geese three times my size, and woof at other dogs and sometimes raccoons. But this tiny duckling knew I wanted to be his friend. I felt proud and puffed out my chest.

Together my daddy and I watched while the duck family loaded into the water one by one, Plink, plink! Plink, plink! Plink!

As they swam off single-file, I thought, *This is the life! Another great day at the lake.*

I hoped we would see each other again, tomorrow.

Sadie's story is donated by Heidi O'Connor. @3phibotticelli

THE FINE ART OF HUMAN RESCUE

My name is Binky Rettstatt and I want to talk to you all about something that is very important for us four-pawed folks. Human Rescue. I know it sounds daunting. But it's an important job and someone has to do it. I mean, look at those poor, lost human souls moping around, lonely and despairing, often with no one to cuddle or who will listen to their woes. That's where we come in. Lest you think your only purpose—whether feline or canine or otherwise—is to throw up on the furniture and lick yourself in embarrassing places at the most inappropriate times, I have good news. You have a noble and, dare I say it, divine calling. You are called to rescue humans.

My first human and I got along okay for a long time. Until *she* came along with her bright smile and allergic kids. Then it was move over, Minnie. Yes, that was my name. Hey, I didn't choose it, he did. In the blink of an eye, I found myself in kitteh jail and with no clue as to what I'd done. Turned out all I'd done was to be a cat—one that shed and made *her* kids sneeze and wheeze. Weaklings. My guy took me for 'a ride,' and I was put in a cage in the corner of a garage at what I later learned was a shelter. It didn't feel that way at first. I was so scared. I was all curled up in a ball, and I'm sure my eyes looked as big as milk saucers. I was so sad and missed my human. He was okay, for a guy, until he turned on me for *her*.

I'd been in that cage for two days when this poor, miserable lady walked in with the shelter worker. My heart picked up just a little bit because, after taking one good look at her, I knew I could rescue her. But she seemed to be more interested in the younger cats. What was she thinking? Those kids would run her ragged, not to mention what they'd do to the furniture.

The shelter worker stopped by my cage and pointed at me.

"What about this one? I'd love to find someone for her."

"How old?" the lady asked.

"We're told she's six."

"Oh," said the lady.

I could tell from her tone, this was hopeless. I looked up at her with the saddest eyes possible, but I didn't think she saw me. I was sad for me, but more so for her because I just knew when she walked in that she was the one for me to rescue.

Well, imagine my surprise when, three days later, the lady came back. The shelter worker pulled me out of my cage. I wasn't too eager to go because I wasn't so sure about strangers, but the lady held me and she didn't even fuss about the hair I left all over her shirt. (I shed a lot when I'm nervous, and I was a wreck.) She put me in a carrier and took me home that very day.

That's when my true rescue work began. I had to make her into a cat parent. I couldn't be too easy on her, so I climbed up the back of the fridge, onto the top of the kitchen cabinets and found a way inside, where I huddled next to the wineglasses. I thought that would show I had class. I squirmed when she wanted to pick me up, and I kept to myself for a while instead of sleeping on the bed with her. If she was going to be a good cat parent, she had to learn to work for it, earn my respect.

It didn't take very long to train her and get her on my schedule. It's important when rescuing humans to establish a schedule and expect them to stick to it. It's also important to play with your human. My favorite game is *Guess what I want for dinner*. And when your human gives up on opening cans and presenting her offering, it's important not to be too easy about giving in. It teaches your human perseverance and patience. Everyone needs more patience, and your human will thank you.

Well, here we are, eight years later. I think it's safe to say I've done a great job of rescuing my human. Her life pretty much revolves around me now, and I can make her smile just with a look. I've broadened her awareness. She actually thinks of me first when she makes plans to travel. (I am so *not* a travel cat and am grateful she understands that.) But I think it's good for her to have me waiting there when she comes home. And she has some really cool folks who look after me when she goes away.

Even when she doesn't feel too good, I manage to perk her up and make her smile. She finds me to be a-mewsing. She's a little neurotic, but I kind of like that about her. It's entertaining, while I'm licking my paws and washing my face, to watch her obsess over something barely worth the time and effort. I just get up on the arm of her chair, pat her on the face and lick her cheek to bring her back to reality. She smiles and kisses my head and I know for sure—my work there is done. For today, at least.

Binky's story is donated by author @Linda_Rettstatt. Employed as Linda's muse/mews, Binky has her own photo page at www.lindarettstatt.com.

RASCAL

My name is Rascal. This is my story. One day I noticed a blonde lady sitting on a porch. I slowly walked to her back screen door and peeked in. When she saw me, she talked to me in a high-pitched voice, asking all kinds of questions that I didn't have answers to, because I'm a cat.

We cats don't give up our secrets to strangers.

When she reached down to pet me, I decided to play bashful, so I ran. Besides not giving up our secrets, we cats like to make humans work for our attention. The blonde lady seemed sad that I wasn't going to make it easy for her, but after she went indoors, I noticed she left the screen door open. Hmmm.

After checking my Stray Kitty Handbook for the recommended amount of time to wait before I investigated, I noticed a flap attached to her sliding glass doors. As I slipped through the flap, I saw two bowls: one filled with water, the other filled with small crunchies that were delicious.

Thinking this was the best place I'd ever found, I decided to explore another room. There I saw a huge square thing that my Stray Kitty Handbook suggested I jump on. Turns out, it was so comfy, and I suddenly felt so tired, that I fell asleep.

Not sure how long I slept, but I awoke abruptly to find the blond lady hovering over me. With no time to check my Stray Kitty Handbook, I flew off the comfy huge square thing and hid. The blonde lady called for me to come out, but my handbook strongly advised to stay put. Besides, I wasn't sure if she was mad because I entered her house without asking purrrmission.

Finally, when the house sounded quiet, my handbook advised it might be safe to come out. I noticed the blonde lady had left the screen door open, so I high tailed it out of there. However, once I was back on the outside, I checked my handbook for what to do next, and realized I'd skipped a whole chapter entitled: Getting Rescued.

Rely on your highly evolved feline instincts, I read. *If human's voice sounds nice, and human has offered you food and a bed, then they have met fifty purrrcent of our requirements to cater to your needs and whims for the rest of your life.*

Hearing the blonde lady calling for me, I thought she sounded nice. And true, she had provided food and water, and that comfy huge square thing for me to nap on.

I stepped out from my hiding place, and she looked so happy to see me, I allowed her to pet me. I was dirty from my life on the road, but she didn't seem to care. In fact, she fed me again, and gave me more clean water to drink.

That night she invited me inside. There I met a cat named Peanut who hissed that she was The Boss. Realizing I'd left my handbook outside, I had to rely on my highly evolved feline instincts in order to win The Boss over. But win her, I did.

I now call that blonde lady, 'Mom.' She says she saved me, but in truth, I'm the one who saved her. And when she named me Rascal, I decided to leave my Stray Cat Handbook lost in the yard for some other cat to use. I didn't need it anymore. I had found my Forever Home.

Rascal's story is donated by Shannon Glarium @3CoolKatz

I AM THE RULER

G 'day. I'm Jazzy, a tortoiseshell princess demanding my spoils in Brisbane Australia. This October 30th I will turn a sprightly thirteen years-of-age, yet only five of those years will have been spent in my current abode with my presently very doting parents.

Prior to my rescue, the parents shared their home with a beautiful little black cat who died at 12 years-of-age while they were away on holiday. Their far more hefty black and white cat had also passed at age 12 the year before that.

Keeping cat comfort in the fore of their thoughts, they decided two more felines would make up their family again, only after air conditioning had been installed. It was important to them that any future cats would live in climate controlled conditions, but also be spared the noise and disruption of the work.

Mum was frantic about finding the two cats who needed her most as she scoured the Internet for cats no one else wanted. Dad admired her commitment, but was scared an older cat would die too soon and make everyone sad again. Mum has depression and Dad tasks himself with managing it. He wanted to protect her from another devastating loss.

Working just five minutes away from the Royal Society for the Prevention of Cruelty to Animals, Mum couldn't resist visiting the adoptable cats in person, talking to staff about the longest residents and who was most in need of a permanent home.

Dad wanted two kittens to give a full, loving and long life to. Mum would only agree to three FIV kittens together, not being able to make the crushing decision of which one should be left behind.

This stalemate meant that, of course, Mum would prevail and the original plan to rescue two older cats was back on the table.

The web showed her two such cats at the RSPCA. A month before the adoption date, my parents visited those two cats. Dad spent time in a cage with one and Mum with the other. Then, with a fortnight to go, they visited again and their decision was made: these two cats would become family. Let me be explicit, I was not one of those cats. I had other plans.

As a wee kitten I was even more irresistibly adorable than I am today. It's no wonder a senior woman seeking feline companionship gave me a home. A home full of pats, scritches and many shared bedtime cuddles. Her penchant for sharing some of her home-cooked meals with me was not unwelcome either. My cozy life was complete. Then the universe delivered the kicker: My loving senior left to wait for me at the Rainbow Bridge.

I was then taken to live with her grandson, however he was not able to give me the life I had become accustomed to. His home contained small boisterous humans, two people sleeping in the big bed, and way too much movement and noise. Plus the focus was no longer on me. Not satisfactory for a princess of my caliber.

Something had to change, and as a cat determined to live according to my Royal station in life, knew how to change it. Once one of the younger, smaller, grabbier humans proved allergic to me, I used my beautiful fur to shed all over the house, thus reinforcing my point that I did not belong there.

These people were not dedicated cat worshippers. Rather than find me a more suitable new home, they left me at the RSPCA like some common cat. There I was forced to share a cage with a long haired bully who hid her true character with one of those cute squishy faces. I knew different, as any exit from my carrier to eat, toilet or just stretch my legs was met with her unjustified aggression. Self-preservation and good princess sense told me to only leave that carrier when dire need warranted.

As a result my nemesis continued to fool the humans into believing we got along as well. My parents, being mere humans, fell for that long haired bully's charms too. In fact, after they met me, patted me, and experienced my gorgeousness, they still kept to their plan to take *her* home with them. What's a girl to do, up against the puny brains of people? Despite their obvious deficits, I knew this couple were my destiny. With such suckers for parents, I would be running their home in no time.

This is when my first owner, watching on from the Rainbow Bridge, intervened. My parents had always planned to adopt two cats. Whilst having the air conditioning installed, the other cat they had chosen to make up their feline duo with the Bully got herself adopted by another.

Finally, utilizing faulty evidence, mum managed to make a sensible decision. Believing just because we shared a cage without bloodshed that the Bully and I must be friends, Mum decided to adopt both of us. Yes. Me—the princess—was the default cat. What a drop in status!

It's hard to look back and describe the trauma we all experienced upon arriving home. The Bully performed to type, showing Mum that I wasn't safe. Distressed by her poor lack of judgment, Mum couldn't stop crying, knowing I was scared; knowing she hadn't provided me with the sanctuary she'd hoped to.

Reflecting back, Mum soon realized that my friendly, loving behavior when she came into the cage at the RSPCA wasn't because I was comfortable with my abode, but because, with her body separating me from the Bully, I was safe to leave my carrier. Mum desperately wanted to give me that safety back.

Seeing that Mum wasn't coping with me being in such distress, and the Bully being vicious and refusing to treat me with kindness, Dad knew this couldn't go on. He convinced Mum to see, as much as she hated to make the decision, her tenuous mental health position couldn't allow her to see me suffer, even if it meant the Bully had to go back. To this day she is disappointed that she couldn't make it work, but I have thanked her a million times for finally making the right choice.

Did I mention before that my Mum is a sucker? The Bully may have been returned to the RSPCA, but my status was not to remain a sole cat for long. Mum still wanted two cats. She thought the last kitten from a litter was a safe choice for me to boss around and guide. Unfortunately Captain Worm-Sparrow does not take direction. Her drum beats very loudly, and she follows it with devout vigor. But the Captain is not mean, just exuberant and she makes our mum giggle, so she's bearable.

Today I am a princess once again. Mum and Dad are devoted

to me, my happiness, my food and my health. I get pats, scritches, air conditioning, the bed, my own cave, a spot on the couch, and a cushioned chair on the balcony to bird watch. As for the Captain, her antics just highlight my class in stark comparison. Hee hee hee!

Jazzy's story is donated by Carolyn Cullen @ClingyCat.

LIVVIE LETS LOOSE

I am Livvie the Rat Terrier. Imagine me speaking quickly in a slightly high-pitched, squeaky voice with a Louisiana accent. That's where I'm from, but my adopted family doesn't know exactly where.

Point of fact: I *do* know, but we have a translation issue. In my language it translates to "the place where the tall grasses grow, and the Feathered Things run."

Years ago, before I finally settled into my Forever Home, my compadres and I used to run free most of the day on a ranch in rural Louisiana. We had some pretty crazy adventures, and one of my pals that I called Tall Cute Boy and I had a lot of puppies, but the humans on the ranch would always take them, and we would never see them again. I felt sad because I love puppies. They don't even have to be mine.

One day Tall Cute Boy, the pups, and I were sniffing around for some hijinks to get into, and we decided to chase the Feathered Things. Maybe we played too hard with them because, in the flash of an eye, we were loaded into a truck and taken some place we didn't recognize, or have a good feeling about. We were separated from each other and put into terrible cages, surrounded by the scent of terror. This terrible place was called a shelter, and it was mind-numbing and nose-numbing. I recall trilling my little bird-like call—a kind of screaming—to find Tall Cute Boy and Little Pups One and Two.

Finally two humans with soft voices took us all in their cars, still in our cages. I never saw Tall Cute Boy again after he and Pup Two went off with one of the soft-voiced humans, and Pup One and I went with the other.

Little Pup One and I were taken on an extremely long ride from Louisiana to a place called Albany, New York. We moved in with a friendly family of humans and dogs and cats. They called me 'Scout.' Or sometimes 'Mama Dog.' And they called Little Pup One, 'Atticus.' He didn't stay with me for long as he soon went to live with a family of soft-voiced humans. I missed him, but I also knew I would soon be very busy as I felt like I had more puppies inside me. I so love puppies, and eagerly looked forward to taking care of them.

Sadly, like all my other puppies, they were soon taken from me. I recall watching a foster sister give birth to her puppies, and asked if I could have some of hers because mine were gone. When she said no, I looked and looked for my puppies, upstairs and down, but I never did find them.

Then, one day my foster mom said, "Mama Dog, you are going to your very own home in Brooklyn." My foster family then drove me to a place they called the Red Roof Inn where I met new humans. We all had fun for a while, but when my foster family left I cried, "Not again!" I was still crying when my new humans offered to cuddle me, and play and talk.

When it was time for bed, I cried a little more because I missed my foster family, and the way I used to sleep with them. I worried I would never again feel safe and comforted. But then my new human said, "Come over here, Livvie." That's when I realized I had a new name: Olivia—Livvie for short. My new human tapped a spot on the bed beside her, inviting me to jump up and cuddle with her. And when she held me in her arms all through the night, I knew I wouldn't have to lose a family ever again. That night in the Red Roof Inn was the beginning of my Forever Home.

I now call Brooklyn my home, and I have a wonderful brother named Kes, and a sister named Twinkle Toes who was a puppy when she came to us. I adore her. I helped raise her like she was my very own. But the best part of my story is, the lady I cuddled with that first night at the Red Roof Inn is still with me. She is my permanent mom. She *is* my Forever Home.

Addendum by Human (approved by Livvie)

Lucky for the dogs, Ratbone Rescue swooped in and pulled all four members of the little family from a high-kill shelter. All were adopted out. Soon after, I became aware of Livvie, and drove to Albany, New York to bring her home to Brooklyn. She showed us her smile right away, along with her penchant for biting noses, but only out of affection.

Livvie came into our household of three other dogs and fit in immediately. She was gentle and kind to our two elderly poodles, and became best friends with Matilda, the greyhound, who helped her learn to be a city pup. Her loving, mischievous personality is a pleasure to be around.

Livvie loves all people with all of her soul. She loves to be held, and hugged to your body. She is a very funny dog, known to make strange, but endearing sounds. And, I'm proud to tell you Livvie has become a Therapy Dog as she is perceptive and healing around people who are sad.

As Livvie has found her Forever Home with me, I can assure you, my heart has found its home with Livvie. She *is* my home.

Livvie's story is donated by Terry Cramer @GigglingR

RAPHAEL'S GREAT ADVENTURE

Raphael the Rescue lives in a very nice house, with cozy beds, soft sofas and chairs, tons of toys and a very loving Mum. Raphael, who had been abandoned as a kitten and had a rough first few months, is deeply grateful to have a forever home. He loves his Mum fiercely and is protectively proud of his house, the property it stands on, and the wild creatures who inhabit the yard and gardens.

Every morning Raphael goes out on what has become 'his' fully-screened porch to survey, as his Mum says, his 'kingdom.' Through the screen he can see the flower beds and trees. He can also see the small ornamental pond which in warm weather has many sorts of frogs who croak and jump, a great curiosity to Raphael: when a frog ventures near the porch, he watches avidly as the peculiar thing hops around in the mulch.

Raphael can also see many different sorts of birds: chickadees, finches, jays, sparrows and wrens, among others. He can also see chipmunks who live in the big rock wall that borders one side of the yard. There are grey and red squirrels cavorting in the many trees on the property, and even the occasional rabbit or hare, nibbling clover in the yard. He's seen garden snakes, mice and voles, deer, wild turkeys, a fox and even a black bear once!

Raphael is content to stay on his porch for hours sometimes in good weather, watching everyone and everything. Most of the visitors to his domain are generally far enough away that they aren't interested in Raphael or his porch: they're focused on other things, like hunting or getting under cover, or chasing each other through the trees, or on any birdseed that might make a handy snack. The birds will occasionally say good morning to Raphael: they know he can't get at them, and so they can afford to be polite. The mice and voles smell the cat, and squeak in alarm and run away.

But the chipmunks stop and stare when they see Raphael on his porch. They know he's behind the screen, and over time they've become so bold that they taunt him. They wiggle their little, striped bodies while Raphael stalks them, whispering, "I could get you. I could. I could grab you..." The more daring chipmunks even tease him, saying, "Ha ha, you can't get me, you can't get through that screen!" But when Raphael switches his tail back and forth and crouches low, his muscles bunched to spring, and narrows his eyes, the chipmunk thinks, "Oops, perhaps you *could* get through that screen!" and runs away.

Raphael's porch is one of the most fascinating, exciting places to be...and because it's screened, he's protected and safe, and Mum keeps an eye on him, too.

Last summer, a strange cat came by one day, trotting up the garden path as though she owned it. Raphael, a friendly, easy-going soul, approached the screen, curious. He had known other cats, of course, on the streets as a kitten and also in the Rescue before Mum adopted him. But he didn't know this cat, and so he waved his tail cautiously, fluffing it out just a bit: no sense in being unfriendly straight off. Before he and the grey tabby could say much of anything, however, his Mum—who had been on the porch with Raphael at the time—jumped up and walked over towards the cat. The tabby saw her, and retreated.

Raphael's Mum didn't know if the grey tabby belonged to someone or was truly a stray, but she told Raphael they would have to keep an eye out for her, and see if they could find out.

A few weeks after that first encounter, the grey tabby returned, but this time, she had three kittens with her: a black and white, a grey tabby...and one who looked just like Raphael, a classic red tabby, or what most people call a 'ginger' kitty. Raphael and the ginger kitten looked curiously at each other through the screen.

Raphael's Mum spotted the tabby and her trio of kittens from a window, and ran outside. Upon hearing the human's approach, the tabby shepherded her kittens away.

31

Raphael's Mum learned from a neighbor that the grey tabby had been dumped a couple of months before, and that she had birthed her kittens under their garden shed. Raphael's Mum set out a humane trap with the help of her friend Sara, hoping to catch the grey tabby and her kittens and get them all neutered. If possible, she wanted to bring them to the Rescue where she'd found Raphael, where they would be cared for and adopted out to good homes.

But all Raphael's Mum caught in her trap was a possum. He had greatly enjoyed the yummy can of cat food she had put in the trap, but he wasn't what she wanted to capture, so she let him go and he trundled away.

The summer waned, and on some clear, cool evenings when Raphael and his Mum sat out on their porch enjoying the sunset and the stars, they would hear the high yipping clamor of coyotes. He did not know what the noise was, but his Mum explained, "They've made a kill. They eat small mammals and rodents...they have to eat, too. Coyotes are very predatory and aggressive, and humans have encroached on their territory," she finished, sounding cautionary.

"I've never seen a coyote," Raphael told her.

"They look like wolves, but smaller," Mum replied, as though she had understood him. "You ever see a coyote, you come inside, Raphael." She sounded a bit stern.

Raphael puffed out the ginger hairs on his chest and wrapped his tail around his paws, sitting up straight. "No coyote better ever come around *my* porch!" he told his Mum proudly, but this time she couldn't have understood him, because all she said was, "That's a good boy."

Time passed, and when most of the leaves were off the trees and the chill winds of early winter had begun to blow, only the ginger kitten—now about four months old—was still around, and he kept to the fields, mostly.

I wonder what happened to the others? Raphael thought. He asked his Mum, but she didn't know, or if she suspected, she didn't say.

Then late one blustery, chilly afternoon Raphael was out on his porch, alone. His Mum had said it was too cold, and urged him to come in. But he could smell winter coming and wanted to enjoy his porch while he could. So his Mum stayed inside, but checked on him every couple minutes through the windows.

Suddenly, Raphael saw an unfamiliar shape slinking through the tall grass in the neighboring meadow. He sniffed the air and opened his mouth, drawing the scent in to try and identify the animal.

It was a coyote! Tan and grey, with pointed ears showing just above the tops of the dry grasses. And it had piercing hazel brown eyes that focused on Raphael with precision. "Mmmm...yummy," the coyote murmured, and licked his chops.

Raphael felt a frisson of fear, and the fur stood up on his back. He fluffed his tail out to its fullest extent and flicked it back and forth in warning. "You, coyote! Stay away from my house! This is *my* territory. Not yours. You may have kits to feed but leave *my* chipmunks and birdies alone. There are tasty voles in the meadow near the fallen ironwood tree," he added informatively, but his tone was stern.

The coyote crouched down in the grass, invisible now, but Raphael knew where he was, and he kept his eyes on the spot.

Then, suddenly, the coyote burst out of the grasses and leapt towards Raphael. Without hesitation, the ginger cat streaked at the coyote, so intent on scaring away the predator that it didn't even register with him when he broke through the screen.

The coyote was surprised: he hadn't expected that. Perhaps this cat was not a cat to tangle with, he thought. He skidded to a stop, turned and ran the length of the yard, veering off into the woods where his pack had their den.

Raphael gave chase until he saw the coyote disappear into the forest. Then, he stopped, and looked around. Where was he? Where was his house? Some kind of big shrub was nearby, and tall trees were a few feet away.

Raphael's Mum must have heard the commotion because only seconds later she stood on the porch in disbelief: a big rip in the screen was flapping in the stiff breeze, and Raphael was nowhere to be seen.

"Raphael! Raphael, where are you?" his Mum called, her voice loud and panicky. Her cat had been out of her sight for less than two minutes, she knew. What had happened? "Raphael!" she called again.

At the bottom of the garden near the tall trees, Raphael heard his Mum calling. "Raphael!" she called again, but then she saw him, and her tone changed from dread to relief. "Come home, Raphael!"

Raphael turned to see his Mum and behind her, he saw his house.

Home! he thought, his heart leaping with joy. That was where Mum was, and where he belonged. Despite the exhilaration of running free with the grass beneath his paws, Raphael sprinted toward his porch.

His Mum ran towards him, and they met right outside the torn panel of screen. Raphael's Mum scooped him into her arms and hugged him. She walked very quickly back inside, into the house. He felt her tears wetting his fur, and next to his, her heart beat fast and hard.

"Oh, Raphael, I was so frightened." His Mum put her nose to his for a kiss. "Whatever made you break through the screen?"

He was very grateful she was not angry, just concerned. He tried to tell her about the coyote, but his Mum was too upset to comprehend.

"I'm sure it must have been very exciting," she told him, wiping her eyes. "But I was so afraid something awful had happened to you, my darling boy." And she hugged him again.

"The coyote wanted to come into *my* yard to hunt," Raphael insisted as he followed his Mum into the living room and sat next to her on the sofa. It never occurred to him that the coyote may have been hunting *him*. "I defended our house and all who live here. I told him to go away. And he did!"

"I'm so grateful you're okay." She stroked his fur gently to make sure he was not hurt. "You're a very brave boy," she added indulgently, but Raphael wasn't sure she really understood.

He was not allowed out on the porch again until his Mum had repaired the screen. She also wrapped metal grating several feet high around the porch, and Raphael knew he couldn't break through that. He also knew that his Mum hadn't really understood about the coyote, how he'd protected her and their house. And how much he loved her.

Fortunately, the coyote seemed to have been convinced that Raphael and his property were best left alone, for he was never seen again.

Now, in the evenings if they hear coyotes yipping over a kill, Raphael gets a reminiscent look in his eyes and he sits up a bit straighter. His Mum may not know what really happened the day he broke through the screen, but he will never forget that he chased off a coyote and defended his home.

Raphael's story is donated by author Deborah Courville.
Writing as Eugenie D. West
http://thebooksofeugniedwest.blogspot.com/
and as Deborah Courville
http://dlc18thcentury.blogspot.com/
Deborah tweets as @RaphaelGingrBoy.

Claudia Monty Freda

TRASH BIN RESCUE

It was 13th March 2005 when I passed the wheelie bins to hear faint meows. I stopped and listened. There it was again!

I located which bin it was coming from and, as the bin was so high, I had to climb into it on top of all the rubbish. When I saw a bag move, I grabbed it and climbed out. It was tied so tightly, I had to rip the bag apart. Out fell three tiny—emphasis on *tiny*—kittens: one ginger, one grey and white and one black and white, not much bigger than mice!

They still had the umbilical cord attached and were damp from birth. Newborns! My guess is they weren't more than one hour old. Any longer in the plastic bag, they would have died.

I put them in a shoebox to take home. As I didn't have kitten formula, I fed them cow's milk through a pipette. I did, however, have a large cat cage and put them in there to take to the Vet who provided me with formula and told me how much to give them. They were bottled fed every two hours, and I was told to rub their tummies with moist cotton wool—as if it were their mother's tongue—so they would wee and poo. The vet told me they had to poo, as any blockage at this stage would be fatal.

At night they were as good as gold. Not one cry. They went to sleep very quickly and, luckily for me, slept throughout the night. In the mornings they all eagerly left the cage when I opened the door, meowing hungrily. These three tiny babies were totally dependent on me, taking up all of my time, and I loved every minute of it. I truly did not expect all three to survive, but ten days later they were still alive. The Vet said that any one of them could die at any time, as it was extremely rare for one-hour-old kittens to survive without their mother. But weeks passed, and they grew stronger, and stronger. The Vet was amazed, and said what a truly wonderful job I had done!

With modesty, I have to agree. Monty, Claudia and Freddie turned 11 years old on March 13, 2016.

Debs Spencer @DebsSpencer1 has donated this story to benefit Four Paws Lifeline.

ROOM FOR MORE LOVE

I grew up with cats. I had my first pair of sisters when I was six-years-old. After the very emotional loss of a twenty-year-old I had raised from a kitten, I didn't think I could handle the pain of losing again, so I went a few years with no cats.

Time passed and I missed the companionship and intimacy of having cats, but still feared the pain of loss. My friend would periodically try to convince me it was time. I resisted. Then one day she sent me a picture of a cat available for adoption. Suddenly, I wanted a cat. Unfortunately that cat got adopted by someone else, but I was lucky enough to connect with a rescuer who had Otis. I had never had a ginger cat, and fell in love. That was six years ago this March. I love Otis more than I can put into words.

I had always had a pair of cats but Otis seemed very happy alone. Periodically I considered adopting another but wasn't sure if it would work for him.

Then…a feral cat gave birth to two kittens in my backyard. The experts I consulted said to keep feeding the mother and leave the babies with her as long as possible. A few days later there were July storms and it was pouring for days. Fearing the tiny kittens would not make it, I went to the spot where I knew the mother cat kept them, but they were gone. Then, my father heard crying during the night and we went outside to investigate. We discovered the two soggy tiny kittens inside a well.

We took them to the animal medical center to be checked out. They were one month old sisters, and needed to be bottle-fed. They also required antibiotics for upper respiratory infections. They had runny eyes that needed ointment, and they had fleas.

My initial intent was to rescue them and turn them over to a no kill shelter, but once I bottle fed them, I fell in love and knew I would keep them. They went from tiny hissing balls of fluff to sweet affectionate babies by the end of the first day.

I have never been so happy for circumstances to work this way. I love my girls, Ruby and Boots, with all my heart, and Otis is gradually accepting and playing with his sisters. I adopted Otis at 11 months because I did not want kittens again, but I'm so happy to be raising these girls. They are so loving and bonded to me. I'm very grateful to have them.

I encourage anyone in a similar situation to adopt. An older cat has the advantage of you knowing exactly the kind of personality you are getting. But kittens are so much fun. There is more room in your heart than you know. While there are no replacements for beloved lost pets, I believe there is always room in our hearts for more love. I am a better person for the animals I am privileged to have in my life.

Otis, Ruby and Boots' story is donated by Lisa Reed.
@LisaReed13

CHAZZ THE DOG

I was living in San Diego County, far away from where my forever Adopted Mom was living in Los Angeles. One day she decided to look at a website for adopting animals. She filled out the form with the pet characteristics that were important to her...and guess what happened? My picture popped out! So she called the contact name and the lady told her they could have me brought very close to where mom lived to meet me.

At that time Mom lived in a different house and had a roommate. She brought him to meet me because, since it was his house, he would have to approve. Well he did. He even installed a special doggie door for me that led to the patio and big backyard.

Mom later told me she took one look at me and thought I was the one for her. When she brought me home, I saw my picture taped to the wall where I could see it. I guess she wanted me to know that I finally had a Forever Home.

A time came when we had to move to the other side of town. No roommates, just me and my mom. Some of Mom's friends say she spoils me with toys, stuffies and such. Well I say they are wrong! I deserve all my stuff and plenty of treats too. I've been with my mom for five years now. I was three when I got adopted and I turned eight last January.

I love living with my mom. We have lots of fun and sometimes she tries to train me. (Snickers behind paw.) Currently she is teaching me the names of my stuffies, and also to put them away when I am through playing. I do it sometimes, but not every time.

BOL. That's Barking Out Loud, for those of you not in the Anipal Twitterverse.

I got pals on Twitter like Herman and Barley. They're both cats, but they're my close pals. They are both extra floofy. My Australian brofur, Thomas Archer, is a herding dog who lives on a farm. He has taught me a lot. I love all my online friends. They are good pals!

Well that's my story...hope you liked it!

Chazz's story is donated by his adopted mom, Barbara Strunin.
@ChazzTheDog1

WHAT CAT LADY'S DO

I first saw her sitting at the edge of the parking lot of my apartment complex. It was a raw morning in early April. She stared at me, feeling safe because of the distance between us. I waved hello because, well, that's what cat ladies do. They greet every cat like they're a friend. As I drove away, headed to work, I checked the rear view mirror. She had disappeared.

That evening when I returned home she peeked her head from under a car a few spaces away. I stopped to talk to her because, well, that's what cat ladies do. They strike up conversations with strange cats. I opened with how pretty she was and this wasn't just flattery. She was a tabby-tort with an off-white muzzle and deep green eyes. She was small but fairly well groomed. I figured she was someone's indoor/outdoor cat. I gave her the slow blink that says to a cat "I mean no harm." She just stared back, not really sure what to make of this babbling, blinking idiot. I crouched down hoping to continue our conversation closer to her level but she bolted for the nearby woods. With a sigh I realized our conversation was over.

I had been without a cat in my home for six months. I had filled out the lengthy form to adopt from the local shelter and been approved but hadn't taken it any further. I was sort of getting used to going away for weekends without the extra hassle of finding a sitter. I didn't miss the extra vacuuming. I hadn't used the lint brush that hung by the front door for months because I knew I wasn't wearing any cat hair as I left the house each morning. Still, I lived alone and sometimes that can get, well, lonely.

For the next two weeks the little cat was in the parking lot every morning when I left for work. She was there each evening when I returned home. Sometimes she sat in plain view, but just far enough away to make a getaway if my slow blinks/no harm turned out to be lies. Sometimes I had to search the parking lot to find her, but she was always there. She began to look a tad shabby and perhaps a little thinner. I began to suspect she had been left behind by some tenant who had moved on. That happened sometimes. So I began to court her in earnest because, well, that's what cat ladies do. I had a vacancy and this was a cat who needed a home.

So I courted her with daily treats in my out-stretched hand, but as her hunger would not override her caution, I had to leave them in a little pile when I left for work. I watched from my rearview mirror as she ate them hungrily. And I persisted in my courtship because, well, that's what cat ladies do. We never accept rejection.

There was a cold, rainy Friday toward the end of April. I had had a horrible day at work. I was angry that I wanted Spring to arrive and it just seemed it would not. I berated myself for not having adopted a cat before now because knowing I was going home to an empty house was totally depressing. I paused in the parking lot, looking for my cat friend but didn't immediately see her. Reluctant to stand in the cold rain any longer I went to check my mail. As I was locking up the mail box I heard a loud and clear "Meow". I looked down and standing at my feet was my little tabby-tort pal with soaking wet fur, and meowing as if to say, "You're late!"

"Well, come on," I said to her and headed for the door. She ran into the building and hurried up the stairs ahead of me. She kept turning her head to make sure I followed. As we climbed the stairs I took the opportunity to discreetly peek under her tail. Yup, a girl, just as I had suspected. By the way, that's what cat ladies do. We never want to call a He a She or vice versa. It's just not respectful.

I unlocked the door to the apartment and she strolled inside like she had been paying the rent all along. I grabbed a towel to dry her soaking fur, but she backed away out of reach. Of course, I thought. I was being much too forward. I was too excited at having successfully courted, and now been chosen. I chattered on, apologizing for being so unprepared to receive a cat.

I went back out into the cold and rain, and drove to Walmart where I raced through the pet aisles, filling my shopping cart with a new litter box and litter, cat toys, a brush, matching bowls for food and water, and of course, oodles of cans of Fancy Feast. At the checkout the lady said, "Looks like someone got a new cat".

"Yes!" I said too loudly, but beaming as I said it because well, that's what cat ladies do. They talk to complete strangers about their cat.

When I got home my new buddy was curled up on the couch. Her fur had dried and she was immediately interested in what was in the bags I had dragged in. The first order of business was to get some food in her scrawny belly. While her head was planted firmly in her new bowl, I set up her new litter box. It felt good that my home was once again cat-friendly.

Once she had eaten she did a quick wash of paws and face, and then came to sit near me on the couch, close but not touching. And she stared at me. And stared. And stared.

I broke the uncomfortable silence with, "What shall I call you?" More staring. So I tried on some names. "Lily?" Staring. "How about Zelda?" More staring. I tried other names. Cassie. Thea. Mariah. All met with the unblinking stare. Running out of ideas I said, "Well, how about Lola? I like that name. What do you think?" And so it was with the name Lola having been spoken, she circled a few times, curled up and closed her eyes. "Lola it is then," I said because, well, that's what cat ladies know. We know when the conversation is over.

I fed Lola once more before going to bed that night. I put the can in the sink, too lazy to rinse it and toss it. I woke once during the night and felt a familiar weight and warmth at my feet. I fell back to sleep with a smile.

I woke the next morning and listened for some sign of Lola. There was only quiet. I stretched and rolled over and felt something strange and hard under my left shoulder. I sat up to find the empty food can I had left in the sink the night before. It had been licked clean and carried from sink to bed and sitting right next to it was my Lola. I laughed out loud. I thought of the scene from Oliver Twist where he presents his bowl and says, "Please, sir. I'd like some more." I practically ran to the kitchen to feed her. It was the earliest I had been out of bed on a Saturday morning in many months because, well, that's what cat ladies do. We never make our kitties beg for food.

That Saturday in April the sun came out and the weather turned warmer. Spring had finally arrived. But I barely noticed because I was so busy getting to know my Lola. In no time we became the best of friends. She let me pat her head and scratch her chin. One day she rolled over and practically ordered me to scratch her belly. She dragged the feather wand to me when she wanted to play. She sat on the window sill and cried for me to open the blinds so she could bird watch.

Nearly nine years have passed since Lola walked into my house. She has grown into a beautiful cat. Silly and playful one minute, regal and mysterious the next. The faintest rustle of the Temptations bag can wake her from a sound sleep two rooms away. Other times you'd swear she's been stricken deaf when I call her for a cuddle that she's not interested in. She's just on the other side of the door each time I come home. I cannot put my purse down or take my coat off until she has been properly fussed over. The vacuum cleaner is the most used appliance in the house. Company coming sends me scurrying with the lint brush and the Swiffer. But I wouldn't trade one minute of my time with Lola because, well, that's what cat ladies do.

They love their cats.

Lola's story is donated by Linda Schmidt @OneInThere

THE RESCUE OF SAINT FRANKIE

Hello, my name is Nutmeg and I want to tell you about my brother, Frankie. In June 2013, Mum saw an urgent appeal online about a little grey cat who was fading fast at the rescue centre. They were desperate to find someone who could foster him right away. He had stopped eating and had completely lost the will to live. Mum already had me, plus my brother, Felix and sister, Poppy, but she didn't hesitate and contacted the rescue centre right away. They were delighted to hear from her and had a good long chat before sorting out a day that they could bring the kitty round to our house.

Well, as soon as Mum saw him she fell in love with him. The nice lady from the rescue centre told Mum that they had picked him up from the streets. Sadly they didn't know his backstory, but it was clear he had been abused and was a very unhappy and scared boy. Mum had adopted the three of us from rescue centres, but had never been a fosterer before. Anyway, she organised a nice room (the kitchen) for him with plenty of bedding, toys and a scratching post. It also had a louvre door, so he could see us through the slats and we could see him, but more importantly he had his own space at all times.

I could tell Mum was keen to adopt him once the initial fostering period was over. He was only known as Grey at the rescue centre, so the first thing she decided to do was to give him a nice name. Her favourite Saint of all time is St Francis, so she thought that would be a good choice. The only downside was that it was a bit formal for a three year old kitty, so she amended it to Frankie.

It wasn't too long before the adoption was formalised, but Mum was careful to take things slowly. It took a number of months before Frankie came out of his shell and Mum knew he would be alright mingling with the rest of us. Frankie is now a very boisterous lad who loves playing with every toy we possess. He loves pouncing on them and leaps straight up in the air and then comes down with a big thud! He and Poppy love chasing each other around the house, and up and down the cat trees, too. It can get very noisy at times, but no one minds because it's so great to see him brimming with confidence.

Frankie's story is donated by Callie Machan @Catgirl321

ONE OF THE LUCKY ONES

Roxy: My story begins like the thousands of other orphaned kitties in Los Angeles, but I consider myself one of the lucky ones. Mine has a happy ending.

To be honest, I don't remember my birth mother too much, or my brothers and sisters. We were born on the streets and it was all my wildcat mom could do to take care of herself, much less the rest of us. She tried her best, but I was always so hungry and it wasn't long before I set out on my own.

It's not easy being on the streets, especially in Los Angeles. I got pretty skinny and my coat was thin. I constantly had to steal food, or stand my ground against the other animals I ran across. I even lost part of a canine tooth in one fight. Eventually I wandered onto a golf course. I figured this would be my new home as there were plenty of places to hide, but it was easy to see anyone coming up on me. Problem was, I was still so hungry.

One day in early February of 2011, I saw food inside a strange looking box. I snuck in but as soon as I took a bite, a door slammed shut behind me. I was trapped in a cage with no way out. Eventually a human came up to the trap. I remember him saying "you're no possum," and he took me to the local animal shelter.

The humans at the shelter were caring and friendly. They cleaned me up and put me in a holding cage. Hey, at least it had a blanket and litter box. Plus I got fed regularly. There were about fifty other cats in the same room as me, and we all got to know each other pretty quick. Every few days there would be a steady parade of humans who would come in and look at us. They'd peer into the cages and maybe take one of my new friends home with them. Me? I got looked at too, but I never really hit it off with anyone. Until that day when I met my future forever mom, Sharon.

Sharon: When my husband and I moved to our new home we felt a cat was what we needed to complete the household. I had in my mind that I wanted a tabby, similar to the one that my sister had, so I started searching for one online. I looked through hundreds of photos and found myself wanting all of them. But when I went to see one at the shelter they were either already adopted or I didn't feel connected to them.

Then one day I saw a kitty named "Betty" online and decided I'd go see her. The staff walked me back to the shelter and pointed to her cage on the top row. When I peered into the cage, this skinny kitty came to the front of the cage and put her paw through the wire bars. I reached out and she licked my hand. Looking at that little face and those big, big eyes... I was hooked. I brought her home and named her Roxy after the music club in Hollywood.

Roxy: I felt the same about Mom. The second I saw her, I knew I was meant to be her companion. There was this other guy who wanted me and I kept looking at Mom, trying to tell her "Please, please don't think about it and give him a chance." I watched her call someone on the phone. I knew if she left I'd never see her again, so I did everything I could to tell her I wanted to go home with her forever. I was so happy when they put me in her carrier.

Instead of taking me straight home, Mom took me to her parent's house where everyone stared at me. I knew what I wanted. I wanted to eat, and I let Mom and her sister know right away.

"Feed me," I said, but they just looked at each other. So I said it again. "Feed me!"

"What's she want?" Mom asked her sister.

"I don't know," her sister replied.

"FOOD," I screamed. "I WANT FOOD!"

"Maybe she wants to eat," Mom said, and they found a few scraps of meat to give me. Hey, no one ever said love was easy.

Eventually Mom took me to my new home. I spent a few hours casing the place, figuring out a few vantage points to monitor anyone coming or going; finding a few hiding spots in case I needed to escape and, most importantly, figuring out where the litterbox was.

At one point I heard Mom on the phone. She said, "We've got a cat! I named her Roxy."

"Who's this 'we'?" I thought. I was under the impression it was going to be just the two of us.

A couple hours later I heard a car pull up. I quickly ran behind the couch just in case it was someone from the shelter come to take me back. But then I heard Mom say, "She's behind the couch," and I saw a man with big blue eyes peer over the edge. I knew right away that this wasn't somebody come to hurt me. It was Dad. I reached up with my paw and tapped him real quick.

"She's so cute!" he said, and he smiled down at me in a way I'll never forget. Ten minutes later I was piled on top of them, purring in joy at my new home and my newfound family.

Sharon: And then you sneezed and the cutest little snot bubble came out your nose.

Roxy: Yeah, thanks, Mom. Thanks for sharing that with the entire world. So anyhow, I spent the next few days figuring out everybody's routine and trying to get them to understand that there were going to have to be a few changes now that I was there. First thing I had to teach them was what they thought was their bed was actually my bed. And that I sleep wherever I want on my bed. Second thing was, that when I say, "Wake up!" – you wake up. And finally, you don't make me wait for my food. I broke into the cupboards a few times when I got hungry and helped myself if they left anything out on the counter. I'll never live down that time when I got busted for licking frosting off a birthday cake.

Anyway, I taught them that running around the house with a shoestring in my mouth meant I wanted to play, and that if I gave 'em a look with my big green eyes, they were to drop everything and pet me for as long as I wanted.

Things were going pretty well, and I was shaping them up pretty quick, but a couple weeks after they rescued me, both Mom and Dad had to leave town for a week. They took me to Grandma's house. Grandma wasn't so easy to train. She was horrified that I was such a wild child, and called me a "holy terror." She would have none of my antics, so she trained me to stay off the tables and counters with a squirt from the water bottle. I learned real quick and am proud to say that I came back from my stay at Grandma's as a well behaved young girl (although I still sneak up on the counters when I think Mom and Dad can't see me.) I still hate water bottles though. Just the sight of one will send me scrambling full speed to hide under the bed.

I've had lots of adventures in the five years since Mom and Dad brought me home, many of which I share with all the wonderful friends and furfriends I've met on Twitter. I've come to love Mom and Dad in totally different ways. Dad protects me and comforts me. I love to ride around on his shoulder while we explore the house together, or snuggle up with him for hours when he's watching the game. Mom is my co-conspirator and also my best friend. She takes me out on my harness to enjoy sunny afternoons in the backyard. I got put into the harness after the time I bolted through an open door and ran away for the night. Apparently they've never heard of a girl's night out for old time's sake! We also play endless games of hunting, chasing and just running around the house. I follow her everywhere and pretty much stay in the same room with her whenever she's home.

Why? Because she's my forever Mom and this is my forever home. I never let her forget how much it means to me that she found me.

To anyone reading this who is thinking about adopting a cat, I can tell you there is one out there right now, waiting for you; hoping you will be their forever companion. We are not low maintenance like common belief. We require attention and much affection. But in turn, we will give you unconditional love and joy beyond imagination.

Roxy's story is donated by Sharon Fletcher. @RoxyRoxLa

LILY

One snowy February weekend we invited neighbors over for a spaghetti dinner. I bought a couple bottles of wine, but instead of putting them in the fridge where the space was needed for appetizers, salads and desserts, I decided to chill them in the newly fallen mound of snow outside my doorwall. I figured I wouldn't keep them out there too long, but long enough that they would be amazingly cold when served.

Shortly before our guests arrived, I went to the sliding glass doorwall to let our spirited yellow Labrador, Lily, outside to do her business. A few minutes later I realized it was getting dark, so I returned to the doorwall to let Lily back in.

To my horror, I saw a streak of yellow flash across the walkway and speed past the edge of the patio. Looking more closely, I saw Lily had one of the bottles of wine in her mouth, clenched tightly by the neck! Blissfully happy with her prize, she ran around the yard like a stallion.

Fearing she might drop it, or bite down, break it, and lacerate her mouth, I calmly (ok, not so calmly) shrieked for her to bring it to me. Luckily, Lily dropped it into a pile of snow as she ran into the house, clearly disappointed that her new found toy was really momma's conversation starter. And what a good one it was.

Lily's story is donated by Carolyn Prentkowski

AN ANTIDEPRESSANT
WITH FOUR PAWS AND A PURR

It's official. I am a mad cat lady. We didn't decide to get a cat. Schrödinger—'Ding' for short—decided to have us. We met him when visiting friends whose cat had just had kittens. Ding strolled over, settled into my lap with a nonchalant air of ownership, and I was lost. After a while I tore myself away from him—I thought I really had better talk to our friends—only to sneak back as soon as I thought I could get away with it. Cue a repeat performance, only this time when I tried to get up, he was so reluctant to let me go that he hid under my skirt. That night my husband and I began to talk seriously about whether it was feasible to have a cat.

Two months later Ding came home and promptly took over our house. He's been the best decision we ever made. I never truly understood the expression 'curiosity killed the cat' until Ding moved in. Although my health limitations mean that sometimes managing the antics of a kitten are less than convenient...

("Ding, I barely have energy to make my lunch. I don't want to get up to stop you knocking things over, or clawing the sofa, or jumping on the kitchen worktop every two minutes.")

...the benefits have surpassed a million to one.

Ding and I discovered afternoon nap cuddles fairly soon after he took up residence. And let me tell you, for someone who has been forced to rest for over a decade, it was a revelation. For instead of resentfully thinking of fun or useful things I could be doing, I instead enjoyed cuddling a bundle of purring fluff.

Now, if I don't have a nap, I miss our duvet cuddles. It's become such a routine that, if I go near the bedroom in the early afternoon but don't go to bed, Ding follows me to sit in the doorway, looking confused. And getting half an hour good quality rest in the afternoon does wonders for managing my health.

This is only slightly marred by my tendency to try and take the perfect 'pet selfie' instead of rest. Cuteness is Ding's superpower.

In an attempt to prevent myself from flooding my Facebook page with pictures of my cat, I created a Twitter account for Ding. I was completely unaware that I was about to travel through a wormhole into the world of Twitter Anipals: an amazing outlet for my imagination and creativity.

I never really grew up. When 'Paddington' came out, I loved it not only for its script and cast etc, but because it let me believe for nearly two hours that the next time I went to London I would find a talking bear that would come home and live with me. So, to find a world—in this case the Anipals—where cats talk, build transporters, pull off bank jobs, have Valentine's dates, and go on multi-continent adventures...my cup runneth over.

I could go on forever itemizing how much joy Ding has brought to me and my husband, but then no-one would read this to the end. Yes, I am a mad cat lady. But Ding means so much more to me. He keeps me company when I'm home alone all day. He distracts me when I'm in pain. He entertains me when I run out of low-energy things to occupy my time. He helps me rest and makes me smile.

Ding has shown me that the most effective anti-depressant has four paws and a purr.

Last Christmas, only four months after Ding came to live with us, I was given several cat-themed presents. My fate is sealed.

I believe from the bottom of my heart that it was part of God's wonderful plan for Ding to choose my lap that day. Ding is a blessing, a gift straight from the Creator who made us both.

Ding's story is donated by Victoria Jane Townsend.
@DrSchrodinger15

I AM RUSTY CAT

This is a story about a sweet little ginger kitty... Wait. That's me! My name is Rusty and I'll be six years old on April 2nd. I was adopted into my forever home on March 2, 2011. My soon-to-be parents weren't looking for a kitty; they were just looking at the kitties up for adoption. They saw a long orange paw sticking out of a cage and came right over to me. Every time they would walk away to look at the other kitties, I would stick my paw out at them. They just couldn't resist my ginger charms.

They got me out of that cage and I sat on a nice warm lap and didn't want to move. They took me home that very day and I'm sitting on Mom's lap right now helping her type. After all, she couldn't write this story without me.

I live in Texas with Mom and Dad, and four other kitties. I have an older brother, Carmelo, who is seven years old and was adopted like me. He's a "Daddy's boy" who always wants to sit in his lap and follow him around. Carmelo and I are both gingers and we get along great. We love to wrassle and chase each other all around the house. Sometimes we knock things off tables but we try not to do that...unless certain things don't belong on the table. Then they get a swipe of a paw and off they go!

Next is a Tuxedo kitty Mom named Mousie; he was born under the deck in our back yard. Mom and Dad do TNR—Trap, Neuter, Release—for any ferals they see in the neighborhood. They caught Mousie when he was a kitten and took him to the vet. He was caged in our house while recovering after his snip-snip (shudders). When they tried to return Mousie outside, he ran back into the house! That was five years ago and he's been inside ever since. We get along really well. He loves to snuggle with me and likes me to give him a bath. Mom says I'm a good big brother.

The next kitties are a brother and sister named Jack and Jill born under that same deck in the back yard about two years ago. Mom says there must be a sign telling all Mama Cats to have their kittens under our deck. Anyway, Mom saw Jack when he was about five or six weeks old. Imagine her surprise when he walked right up to her and let her pet him and pick him up. She couldn't believe it. Dad came out and Jack went right to him, too. This little kitty was never afraid of humans. Jack got the snip-snip and the same thing happened, like with Mousie. They tried to put Jack outside, but he meowed and scratched at the back door to come inside, and he's still inside with us now.

Last but not least is our little sister, Jill. When she first came out from under the deck, she was sneezing a lot. She was spayed, and given medicine. She is a very sweet kitty who has also stayed inside with us, however she prefers only Mom to pet her.

We all love to snuggle and nap on Mom's and Dad's bed. There is a towel at the end of the bed and all five of us sleep on it. We all like Temptations treats and whenever Mom or Dad shakes the treat bag, we all come running. In fact, when they say "Treat," we know what they're saying and meow at them. We have an awesome cat condo we like to nap in too. My favorite toy is a nip mouse that I carry around and play with a lot.

Living in the hot state of Texas means we don't have many 'open window' days. Fortunately, it's been so nice these past few months that we've enjoyed open windows almost every day. Mom says don't get used to it though, because the temps will be in the 100's before long. But for now, whenever we hear the windows being opened, we all run to them so we can look out at the birds and all the ferals.

Oh! I haven't told you about all the ferals Mom and Dad take care of. Let's see, in order of when we first saw them and they're still around: Blackie, Meow-Meow, the three triplet kitties called Trippers 1, 2 and 3, Pumpkin, Autumn, Snow Paws, Mama Kitty, Cricket, Pepper and Cinnamon. There have been many others, but they didn't stay around. There were brothers called Left Sock and

Right Sock, sisters Mary Ann, Ginger and Professor, and sisters Ying and Yang. Mary Ann still shows up from time to time, but we have not seen the others in a long time.

As you can tell, my Mom and Dad have cared for lots of kitties over the years. In the winter, they leave the garage door cracked open for Blackie and some of the others to come inside. There are beds, blankets, food, water and a litter box in there so they stay warm and comfy when it's freezing outside. I think Mom and Dad have a soft spot for kitties. Lots of the ferals even rub against their legs and get pets and chin scritches. They know they are loved and they return the love.

My Mom works full-time and Dad is retired. Mom runs marathons and Dad says she's nuts for doing that; she says she would be nuts if she DIDN'T run! She enjoys it and has met lots of great friends while she trains and runs the races. She keeps saying she wishes I would go out and run with her, but I'm with Dad. I'd really rather not.

I joined the Twitter Anipal community on August 13, 2011 and am a member of #wlf, #wlfTX, #BBOT, #NASCARAniPals. I'm proud to be the drummer in the band @Feral_Beast. I'm also Chef for #Brekkieclub. I love all my pals on Twitter and enjoy spinning tunes at parties, making delicious brekkies and tweeting with them.

Hope you have enjoyed reading about me and my family. Take care and I hope to tweet with you soon. *runs off to play with nip mouse*

Rusty's story is donated by Elizabeth Culver. @IAmRustyCat

WORKING FOR DEANO AND TASHA

When I found myself stalking neighbourhood cats on my way to and from work, seeking feline approval, or at the very least, feline disdain meant only for me, I knew it was time. I needed to own a cat and get that special brand of disdain in the comfort of my own home. I vowed to only get one cat because I knew the slope of feline ownership was a slippery one and I did not strive to be the featured character in any comic strips, cartoons or memes.

I started my research and noticed Tasha featured on an animal clinic's adoption page. When I saw her sweet face and read that she was described as lazy, I just knew I could give her a loving home. Being lazy myself, I felt we would be perfect together.

When I contacted the clinic to express my interest, a staff member advised me that they could not hold Tasha for me. Another woman was also interested in her and was coming to the clinic the same day I intended to visit. Keeping this in my mind, I asked my mom, my sister and my nephew to serve as part of the selection committee; this was an important decision and I needed input from my future cat sitters. When I arrived at the clinic, I saw that Tasha was as adorable as I imagined, but I also knew that she was likely to get her forever home soon, given that someone else had inquired about her.

In the corner, a distinguished looking Lynx Point Siamese had risen to his full height to survey the herd of besotted humans who had entered the room. A staff member informed me that Deano was not featured on the website because he had not been in the shelter long enough to be profiled. He obviously knew lovesick fools when he saw them, and he used his stature to his full advantage. His beautiful blue eyes worked their magic and I knew my decision had been made for me. The selection committee agreed that Deano was the feline I should welcome into my home, as clearly, he had already claimed a place in my heart.

Deano rapidly adjusted to being the king of his castle. He loved being petted while assisting me with my marketing and planning. Most of his evenings were spent curled up with me on the couch; he appeared deeply satisfied with the life he was living. The first time I had to leave Deano alone so I could attend a conference, I worried about how he would do in my absence. It was now March and Deano had been with me since January. When I arrived home after the conference, I soon realized that Deano missed me a great deal. After he launched himself from the top of the fridge onto my shoulders, clinging to me like I was a life preserver saving him from drowning, I considered adding another cat to our family.

I took some time to consider whether or not bringing another cat into the house was a wise decision. I was Deano's person and he happily monopolized my lap and my time. While I deliberated what I should do, I was compelled to visit the animal clinic website where I first spotted Tasha. To my dismay, Tasha's picture was still featured as a cat waiting for her forever home. I knew in my heart that I couldn't let her down again. She knew Deano from his time at the shelter and I felt this could be an advantage when I introduced her into the house. My decision made, I contacted the clinic and made arrangements to get Tasha that weekend.

When Deano and Tasha were first reunited, it was not the heartwarming scene I had painted in my mind. Deano was openly jealous and not fond of sharing his only human with the new interloper. I immediately sensed that Tasha could not believe she was going to be living with the high-maintenance pretty boy she had first encountered at the shelter. Deano quickly informed Tasha that my lap was his and her place was on the back of the couch, or better yet, another room in the house. Fortunately, after several rounds of kitty wrestling, Tasha and Deano eventually developed a relationship that worked for them both. They were bonded by their common goal of training me to be a competent employee. They both agreed that I would no longer establish the rules in the house; my job was to pay the mortgage, buy the food and be on-call constantly.

It soon became obvious I worked for them now; they vowed to continue my training until I no longer disappointed them and I vowed to do better each day. If I am lucky, and can find just the right treats, my next performance review might not contain a list of recommendations for improvement longer than a typical doctoral dissertation!

Deano and Tasha's story is donated by Shauna Gibb. @SGibb1

GRISSOM

I love it when Grissom "trades" me. Tonight he wanted my dinner. As I'm eating he searches through his toys and chooses an old chew he's been working on lately. He brings it to me and places it in my lap, then steps back; looks at my plate, then at the chew, then at the plate and licks his lips.

It's going to take me a long while to get through this chew. I love my boy.

Nine years ago, I rescued my love. Seems like we have been together forever. I had wanted a Spinone for years, but could never afford one, so I put my name on a rescue waiting list. It took over three years to be called.

I took my daughter, Jenna, with me to take a look at this older dog. As we drove onto the breeder/rescuer's property, I saw she had a pen full of puppies, ready to go. Cute, wiggly little puppies! I so wanted a puppy. But then they brought out the older dog, called 'Caesar.' Jenna put a leash on him and off they ran into the nearby field. Meanwhile, I played with the puppies. Maybe I could scrape money together and buy one after all. What to do? I had to make a decision by the time Jenna and Caesar returned.

A half hour later, I saw them emerging from the field, both panting with huge grins on their faces. No decision was necessary. Caesar made my daughter laugh. He nuzzled me and pushed his face into my leg.

As we opened the back of the Jeep, he leaped in and Carol, the rescuer was in tears. She told me Caesar had not shown any interest in people since she had found him. He had shut down from the abuse and abandonment he had suffered at the hands of his original owners. In fact, he had not even interacted with the other dogs. But Carol saw him come to life with us.

I renamed him Grissom. New life, new name. He took to his new name immediately.

Nine years later, we have been through so much together. No eloquent words can adequately tell you what he has done for my heart.

I've only received one kiss from him, the day my Dad died. Grissom sat close while I sobbed, and I felt him gently kiss my cheek. It was what I needed. He always gives me what I need.

I constantly tell him what he means to me. I brush him, play with him; take him to the park and to the vet. When I come home from work, he does this ridiculous "Happy Dance" with over 100 pounds of Spinone bouncing up and down, and leaping into the air. It's a sight to behold and it's all for me.

In the evening he will stand quietly, and make a soft moo sound. Yes, like a cow. When I ask if he wants to 'snuzzle,' he will run at me, full force. I sit at the edge of the couch and he will push his nose into my neck and take long breaths—like he's trying to memorize my scent. I rub his ears, face and back as he breathes me in.

Grissom now plays with others, greets humans, though somewhat cautiously, and lives a pretty good life. He takes orders from my cats, sleeps in my bed, and has his own couch. He protects me from men in hats and little girls who scream in front of our house. I put his needs before my own. There is nothing I wouldn't do for him.

Grissom has enjoyed a fuller life since he rescued me. He's met and played with former Detroit Tiger baseball pitcher Milt Wilcox. He's had his picture in the newspaper and across the internet. He has participated in Meals on Wheels for Pets, and attended many pet events and parties for Halloween and Christmas. I've thrown him birthdays parties complete with doggie cake. He's had his paw print in clay, and donned a pink hair weave in support of Pet Cancer Awareness. My boy has done it all. Yes, I rescued him and he rescued me right back.

Grissom lives to make me laugh and feel loved, and in return I make sure he is healthy, happy and loved. It's a win-win situation. Nine years ago my life changed. Who would have thought adopting an older dog would have been one of the best decisions of my life? Think this story is too much ado about a dog? Tell me, have you ever been loved unconditionally? Everyone deserves this type of love, whether man or beast. Wouldn't the world be a better place?

Grissom's story is donated by Janice Robinson.

MASTER TABBY-WAN

Hi! Connor here. Most of you know me as Master Tabby-Wan (aka MTW) on Twitter. This the story of how I came to live with the human I now call Mom.

At 18 months old my sister Pepper and I were brought to a shelter. Luckily we got put in a cage together. I wondered if we would find a home. Then a guy stopped by our cage and called some of the others over. "Look at these cats, he said. "Look at their cool markings. They look like a snake."

Well, they wanted to see the male cat, and that's me, so I was brought to a room where we could get to know each other and see if I would be a good fit. I knew I would be, but you know humans. They like to figure things out for themselves. And since humans can be somewhat unpredictable, I knew I had to give them a push in the right direction. So I reached up like I wanted to be picked up, and the lady put me in her lap. She was nice and I liked her, so I purred, doing my best to convince her I should be adopted. I have to say I forgot myself for a minute and did bite, but it was just a love nip. I swear! Then I went back to being good.

It worked! I was chosen to go home with her. Actually Mom says I chose her, and she was right.

They gave me a blue collar, and then put me inside a box. I don't like being confined, so I meowed to be let out. When they ignored me, I meowed louder. And louder! Once we were in the car I heard someone say, "Let him out of the box." When the box opened I stuck my head out and looked around. When I spied my new mom, I jumped out and crawled into her lap. Suddenly overcome by my big day, I quickly fell asleep.

I woke up as we arrived at my new forever home. I was so happy, I ran all over the place. There was so much to look at and smell. Plus I wanted to pick the best place to hide because you know that's what we cats like to do. I found a perfect place behind the bed, but then my new mom arrived with a bag of treats, and we all know how much I love treats, so my hiding spot was quickly uncovered.

As my new family could only adopt one kitty, I missed my sister Pepper for a while. I hope she found a good forever home, too, like I did. But that was many years ago.

In July I will celebrate my 17th birthday with my Mom and Grandma. I expect to get a toy and treats on that day, but the best present is the one Mom gave me those many years ago when she promised to take care of me. She not only took good care of me— she took *great* care of me.

Connor's story is donated by Tami Schipper. @MasterTabbyWan

CHEVY

My name is Chevy, and this is the story of how I started life as part of an unwanted litter, and found myself rescued. By anyone's estimate, I was born around the end of July or the beginning of August to feral cat parents. Early one morning when I was a few weeks old, I got the bright idea to wander out of my nest to explore.

The sun was hot that day, and the pavement even hotter. I soon regretted my decision to scamper from the safety of my nest where I had my kitty mommy and my littermates. I was alone, lost and scared. I was also hot and so tired that I crawled into a cool place to rest. To my horror my cool place to rest was noisy and also moved very fast. I hung on as best I could until I stopped moving. I would later find out that my cool place to rest was the engine bay of my future Daddy's car.

After a short time, I heard humans approach. Suddenly I was surrounded. I had never seen so many humans in one place before. I later learned I had taken refuge from the heat inside a car that had driven to a garage for a car inspection. When the hood opened, I saw a bright light and figured life as I knew it was over. There I was, up close to people I had never seen before, and I was so scared that I jumped and ran as fast as my tiny legs could carry me...straight into the mechanic's tool chest.

Fortunately the men who worked there were all very nice. They shut down the garage until they could fish me out of the tool chest, and put me into a small box to hide in. My future Daddy hadn't come to a car inspection prepared to become a kitten Daddy, but he took it well, thank goodness.

The next thing I knew, I was back in the car on the front seat next to the guy, and on my way to his home. I'd never had a home of my own, so I was scared. All I knew of life so far was the outdoor nest where my kitty mommy and my siblings lived. I'd wanted to explore the world just outside the nest, and just look what had happened! I did not feel very good about this turn of events, not at all. I shook with fear and cried, and tried to escape, but it was no use. I could not open the lid to that box.

When the man who would become my Daddy presented me to the woman who would become my Mommy, I hissed, spat, carried on, and tried to hide behind a desk. The woman caught me, pronounced me wild and cute, and then said the shot clinic at the Humane Society was open that day, and they could test me for kitty diseases, tell how old I was, and get me on a shot schedule. After that, she said, we would work on this hissing stuff.

I wound up back in the box, and back in the car, again! What is it with humans and cars? The Humane Society was scary and very noisy. After I suffered through my first-ever examination, I was declared to be about 4 weeks old, and healthy—although dehydrated and clearly hungry.

On our way home, my new parents bought me formula and a nursing syringe, among other things made just for us kittens. When we finally returned home, I was exhausted from being hungry, thirsty and scared; not up to my usual feistiness to struggle, much less hiss or spit. While Daddy held me, Mommy mixed the formula and offered it to me. Of course I refused. I wasn't going to make this easy for them. Then Mom noticed something the vet had not: black dirty stuff that had plugged up my nose. I couldn't smell anything. That's why I wasn't eating. Kittens that can't smell, won't eat.

The next thing I know, Mom put me into the sink, and I got scrubbed from head to tail to get all that nasty dirty stuff off of me and out of my nose. I protested with all my might, but it was no use. I was getting a bath, and that was all there was to it. Finally, I was not only healthy, but I was clean, and wrapped in a warm, dry towel. For the first time in my life, I felt great!

Then Mommy tried feeding me the formula again. I cautiously tasted it…and I liked it so much, I ate every drop. When there was no more formula in the syringe, I was so mad, I threw a little hissy fit. And I kept hissing until Mommy fed me more formula. With a very full tummy, I drifted off into a deep asleep.

When I woke up, I found myself in Daddy's office where it was safe and warm and dry. So comfortable. Mommy and Daddy made me a little nursery box with a soft bed in it, and just outside of my nursery, there was a dish of water and a litter box—just my size. As I didn't know about litter boxes yet, my first piddle in my new home was done in my water dish, which got me put back in the sink for a butt bath, but I sure enjoyed that warm soft towel.

After my second bath, I was hungry again, so Mommy fed me more of that yummy formula. This time Daddy put me in the litter box right after I ate. Suddenly a light went on in my head, and I used my litter box to piddle in. I felt like a champ when Mommy and Daddy cheered, and told me that I was a really good kitten. I then returned to my nursery with my very own soft bed, and slept for a really long time.

When I woke up, I was hungry, so I cried, knowing Mommy would come to my rescue. She made me more formula, and while I ate, she stroked my fur. I decided that I liked being stroked so much that, after I finished eating, I headbonked her face over and over. I also practiced my purring. Mommy kept stroking my fur. I kept headbonking her and purring. And when Daddy woke up, I practiced headbonking and purring on him, too. That was apparently a good thing for me to do, because they kept telling me what a very good boy I was.

I've lived with my Mommy and Daddy, and my brofurs, Leo and Lou, for over a year now, and I'm proud to tell you I have transitioned successfully into a happy, healthy house cat.

Chevy's story donated by Sass MacConney @LiveLoveMeow

THE DOG WE DIDN`T KNOW WE NEEDED

Never in my wildest dreams did I imagine ever having a dog, yet our household is now home to one. It's not that I didn`t like dogs. I liked all of our friends' dogs, and never denied petting and belly scratches to any dog wanting them; but I never *loved* dogs. They`re so very different from cats. They're big and clumsy. They bark instead of purr. They are dependent, and they have to be walked and picked up after. And they smell like, well... Dogs.

I had just pulled into the parking lot at my Mom's nursing home when my cell phone rang. It was my husband Bill with a question I wasn't expecting. "Can I have a dog?" Over the years, he had talked about getting a dog, maybe a rescue greyhound, maybe a Chihuahua he'd call El Diablo. The conversation was always the same. If we get a dog, he would have to be the one to feed it, take it outside for potty; take it for walks, and scoop up after it. The conversation would always end there. As someone who had a hard time scooping out the cats' litter boxes, the idea of following behind a dog, ever ready with the plastic bag was a deal-killer for Bill.

A former work acquaintance, now working for the Humane Society of Wisconsin in Milwaukee, also remembered Bill's conversations about adopting a rescue greyhound and had given him a call. He repeated the conversation to me: a litter of puppies that needed homes. Driven up from Louisiana in a truck. If he wanted to look at the puppies, he'd need to do it that day.

Can he have a dog? My answer was the same as always. I wasn't going to say he couldn't have a dog. Once again we went through the conversation of the past...nighttime trips outside, daily walks, scooping poop. Was he ready to own a dog?

At that point he wasn't sure, and still had many unanswered questions. He'd just go and look. With those words, I flashed back to the day I stood in front of a cage at a cat show. In the cage was a breeding quality bluepoint Himalayan female kitten. "But I don't want a breeding quality cat, I just want a pet," I had said to the breeders. "Just pick her up and hold her," was their reply. As if she was trained to do so, the cat rubbed one side of my face then the other. She made "kitty biscuits" with kneading paws, and she purred. I went home with a breeding quality Himalayan kitten.

For the record, "just go and look" is also how we bought our first car, a sailboat and our first house. I know what happens when you "just go and look."

I arrived home about 10pm that night, tired after spending a total of four hours driving, and a full day with parents. As I walked to the front door I could see a large box through the window. It read *Lifestage* crates. I thought it, but yet didn't really believe it: *We're getting a dog.*

I walked into the kitchen. There was a bag of puppy food on the counter. Again in disbelief I thought, *We're getting a dog.*

I looked down, and there on the floor was a food dish, with food in it. Oh my God. We HAVE a dog. It still didn't seem real. I turned around to see Bill holding an eight pound silver and black ball of fluff. It was real. This was our *gulp* D-O-G.

Bill told me the ball of fluff's name was Charles, and he was born on November 13: Bill's birthday. Can you say kismet? Also, Charles was a Catahoula/Lab mix.

A what? Time to go online.

Catahoula. Catahoula Leopard Dog. Catahoula Cur. Catahoula hog dog. Indigenous to North America. Named for Catahoula Parish. Also introduced into the breed were Irish Wolfhounds and Bull Mastiffs. Boar Hunters. Raccoon hunters. Cattle herders. Active dogs...it would be good if they could herd cattle for an hour a day...

Marta—the breeding-quality Himalayan cat—would *not* enjoy being a cattle herd substitute.

Males often reached 90+ pounds. The Humane Society estimated 40 to 50 pounds.

My God, what had Bill gotten us into?

The pup would need a new name. As he was from Louisiana, ideas of Cajun, swamps, bayou, Voo Doo and New Orleans themed-names came to mind.

Back to the Internet to Google "Cajun dog names" where the list was quickly narrowed to Andouille, Gris Gris, Ju Ju, Gumbo and the eventual winner: Gator.

The early days were spent turning the living room into a large puppy pen with all furniture pushed to the wall, and whatever table we could tip on its side to become the doggie barricade. Bill made many a night time trip out into the cold, and we learned that during the evening, even taking a puppy out once an hour was not enough.

That first week we spent an evening with a trainer learning the basics, and made two hour visits to PetSmart to buy toys and to let Gator meet other dogs. When he was old enough, we started Puppy classes. After driving by it for years, we made our first trip to the Dog Park.

We settled into Life with a Dog. We learned to read his cues: when he was hungry, when he needed to go out, when he was overtired, and it was time for the crate. And he settled into ours: day times at the office with Bill, evenings at the dog park, then snoozing at our feet after supper.

We watched him grow too. One week after getting Gator, we had to go out of town (planned prior to adopting him). We were amazed to see that after only two days away, the round little fluff ball had sprouted legs! Then the body followed. This pattern continued until the 40-50 pound estimate was reached...and *passed*.

Gator's territory expanded from the living room to the entire house, much to Marta's chagrin. And when he was no longer allowed to go to work with Bill, and we were able to trust him home uncrated, his world expanded by way of a doggie door that would open when his collar transmitter was close enough. Once outside, he had 2-1/2 acres of lawn and prairie to roam.

As he got bigger and the weather got better, after-work trips to the Dog Park became a daily activity, walking with what amounts to the dog version of a playgroup. And as the summer grew hotter and drier, kiddie wading pools (two of them) were bought, and we took him to the dog beaches at nearby state parks.

We've watched Gator grow from a ten pound bundle of fluff into a gangly puppy, and now into a handsome seventy pound dog. We've seen him change from excitable puppy, to the "teenager" testing the limits of obedience, to the sweet and gentle dog he is today.

Gator came into our lives at a time when I was rarely home. I was either working long hours trying to meet production goals that would allow me to keep my job, or spending time with aging parents who needed help. Bill needed more in his life than coming home to an empty house and watching TV.

Several months after we adopted Gator, I lost the job I'd had been at for twenty years, and for the first time in my life, I had nowhere to go, and nothing to do. I would have had no desire and no reason to get out of bed in the morning, except I had a dog and that dog needed breakfast and needed to be walked.

Once daily trips to the Dog Park became twice daily trips, Bill and I got to know other dog owners, and it became as much a social activity for us as it was for Gator. It became the best part of our day.

Gator will never be as streamlined and elegant as the cats. I'd still rather hear a 5am purr than a 5am bark. Toys need to be picked up in the house *and* yard. And yes—he smells like a *dog*. But we can't help but smile when we see his doggy grin and excited dance every time we turn into the driveway.

I never imagined I would ever have, or even want a dog. Yet now I can't imagine not having him. Life is good for Gator and Gator is good for us. He`s the dog we never knew we needed to have.

Gator's story is donated by his mom, Laura. @RealFakeGator

ANDERSON'S STORY

It was winter. I'm not exactly sure of the date. January? February? January, I think. Mid-January. All I know for sure is that it was cold, there was a lot of snow on the ground, and it was not a good time for a cat to be out on his own in Canada.

And I was hungry. I was so very hungry. I've heard people joke about feeling like they're 'starving,' but most people have no idea what that really means. What it's like to have no food in your tummy for so long that it literally aches. To not remember when you last ate and not know if you'll ever eat again. I know exactly how that feels.

The thing is, when the ground is covered with snow, a cat can't catch mice to eat because the mice are all asleep in their homes underneath the snow. A cat can't even catch a bird because you can't run fast enough through the snow to catch them. Your paws sink into all that fluffy white stuff, slowing you down. The only food to be found are scraps thrown out with garbage and even those can be hard to come by. And sometimes when you *are* lucky enough to find a good garbage can, people will chase you away. They'll yell at you and throw things. You learn to be very wary of people. Better safe than sorry, as they say.

So that's how I had been living for a very long time. I was terribly thin from hunger and so very cold. I was miserable. I wasn't living the good life, I can assure you.

You'd think I would have wanted a better life for myself. One where I could be inside and warm and well fed. You'd think I would have sought out a family so that I could have all those things, but no. You see, I was terrified of people. Absolutely terrified. I wouldn't let anyone near me. I didn't even want people to *see* me.

No matter how rough my life was, I knew better than to trust human beings. Or so I thought.

Then came that day in mid-January. The first day of the rest of my life.

Quite by accident, I came across a house where a number of cats lived with two people, but by no means was I willing to trust those two people. They were *humans*, after all, and I knew better than to trust humans. But the other cats didn't seem afraid of them. The other cats seemed to even like them. Still...

The best I could do was allow the humans to feed me. Now I say that as if I was doing them a favour by eating the food they put out. I know that's not really true. I do realize that the people were *helping me,* and that I really did need their help. I know that. But you have no idea how scared I was of them. I was so scared that even though I needed their help, I was too terrified to take it.

Eventually, we came to an agreement, those people and I. They would put out dishes of food every morning and night, and then scurry back inside the house before I spotted them. They knew they had to put the food out before I came looking for it, for if I caught a glimpse of them, I wouldn't be back for the rest of the day. They came to be quite good at making sure the dishes were there, waiting for me, and for the first time in a very long time, my tummy stopped aching from hunger.

A month passed. Then two. It was still cold but the days were growing longer and the sun, warmer. It was a good thing, too, for my long fur had become very matted and on one side, it began to peel off. Peel off! I had one giant mat on my right - I *think* it was my right - side and it peeled off just like a sheep being shorn. Just to be clear, I don't actually know about shearing sheep, but I've been told that that is exactly what it looked like.

Sometimes, when the sun was shining in the afternoon, I would head to the back of the house and climb onto the deck. There I could often find a clearing in the snow and lie down on my side *with* fur, allowing the sun to warm my bare skin that was exposed. I knew the people in the house were watching me through the window, for more than once I heard them whispering about how I must be a feral kitty. Only a feral kitty would be so scared as to not allow them to help him more. Only a feral kitty would rather stay outside in the cold with all that bare skin than to brave the people indoors.

By spring, I was beginning to feel a little better about the people. Just a little, mind you. They still weren't getting anywhere near me. I made sure of that. But if I were to arrive and find no meal waiting for me, I was now willing to sit and wait for it—at a safe distance, of course. After I was absolutely positively sure that the people were safely back inside the house, I would approach and eat the food they had given me.

By mid-summer, the fur on my side was growing in quite nicely. In fact, you could barely even tell anything had happened to it. I was actually looking pretty handsome. Still a little on the thin side, but I was really turning into a very good-looking cat.

I was starting to trust those people a lot more, too. I no longer ran at the sight of them. I still kept my distance, but no longer ran.

Then came late summer and believe it or not, I started approaching the people. Sometimes I would come right up to them as they were placing my dinner on the ground. A couple times, I even touched my nose to a human hand. This was, of course, by accident and on those rare occasions, I let the people know, in no uncertain terms, that they were to be more careful in future. I let them know by fizzing. Oddly enough, the people weren't scared of my fizzes. In fact, I think I once even caught one of them suppressing a laugh.

Then on Friday, September 26th of 2014, I did the unthinkable. To this day I have no idea what possessed me to do what I did. Never in my life did I ever think I could do such a thing, but on that day in late September, I walked into the house.

One of the humans quickly closed the door behind me, but she needn't have. I wasn't scared. I was *home*.

Believe it or not, I even allowed her to pick me up and carry me further inside. Everything just sort of clicked inside my head. It was like I suddenly remembered what it had been like to have a home and a family who loved me. What it was like to be warm, inside, in the winter and have enough to eat so that my tummy never hurt from hunger. I just *remembered.*

I spent the next two weeks living inside that house. In fact, I moved right in, upstairs. Yes, I headed upstairs to where the bedrooms were and settled right in. The people had to get a new litter box up there - for my very own personal use - along with a tray for my food dishes. By the middle of October, I was feeling a lot more secure and started coming down to the kitchen to eat with the other cats, and by the end of the month, I was even willing to go outside again and play, always coming back in to eat and be cuddled. I had become one of the gang.

Then they took me to be neutered. We won't talk about that except to say, from what I understood from the other cats, once the people get you neutered, *you know you're in.*

The people - who are now *my* people - realized I had never been a feral kitty at all. They realized I must have been abandoned at some point, and then terrorized by humans when living out on my own, for a truly feral kitty would never have adjusted to living inside so quickly, if ever at all.

Now I'm *living the life of riley,* although to be perfectly honest I no idea who this Riley guy is, nor why I'm living his life. But it's a good life. I have a home, a family who loves me, food in my tummy and I'm never left outside in the cold. What I went through is all in the past and my future looks good.

Anderson's story is donated by Jennifer Niemi. @NerissaTheCat

PIE ~ THE FAT CAT

I am born – Monday 30 Oct 2000. The headline in the paper read 'Britain hit by worst storms for 13 years.' Winter was rapidly approaching and the squally storms of the jet stream had brought treacherous weather conditions.

In the early hours of that morning, my mother gave birth to us under the meagre shelter of a hedgerow in Haslington, Cheshire. There were four of us kitties. We were so lucky to survive. The ditch next to us was flooding rapidly and as we were only a few hours old, we were getting colder and weaker. I doubt we'd have survived another twenty four hours. It was extreme weather - blustery, driving, relentless rain. It must have made my mum quite worried trying to keep us all together and alive. My mum wasn't the brightest cat on the block. (I think I've inherited her intellect at times. My sister must take after my dad as she is quite clever.) I never met my dad. He's out there somewhere, probably haunting the Cheshire plains. I'll bet his 'Cheshire cat' grin endures though.

Later that morning, as the grey dawn arrived, Sandbach Animal rescue received an anonymous phone call. They spent some hours searching for us all. Luckily they found us and took us back to recuperate, sheltering in a dark, cosy, warm barn filled with straw and cardboard boxes. That's where my early kitten days were spent. I didn't have a great deal of interaction with humans at this stage. It has affected my ability to accept strangers a little, but I've improved vastly over the years and gained confidence by plenty of gentle exposure to kind folk along the way.

Fourteen weeks later, still in a dark barn somewhere in Haslington, when we were getting confident and boisterous, we started to have lots of human visitors. Families would call in, play with us for a few minutes, but then they'd leave again. Finally, during one of these visits, I was clamouring out of a cardboard box with my wobbly legs and someone lifted me onto their knee. I mewed softly and I must have impressed them as I was chosen! They adopted me and my sister and we went to live in Nantwich in a fascinating old black and white house full of nooks and crannies.

For the first few months we weren't allowed out, and I had to use a series of litter trays which escalated in size as we grew. We learned the rules of the household and soon settled in. We were both delighted with the amount of toys and play areas we'd been given. I think we did our best to amuse our family as they did seem to laugh with us quite a lot. My favourite toys were cotton buds out of the bathroom which triggered my 'pouncing' reaction, and I loved playing with them. My sister decided she like black spidee's the best. She still prefers them to other toys to this day.

When I was less than a year old I had a couple of minor 'accidents' on the human's bed. I did 'widdle' twice right in the middle of a white king-sized duvet, but that was a mistake. When I realised it wasn't 'grown up' to do that sort of thing, I was upset with myself because I'd done the wrong thing, but I was instantly forgiven and soon learned the difference between a soft duvet and a cat litter tray.

When Spring finally arrived, we were allowed to start our outdoor adventures. We played out on the dewy grass in our own private backyard. It has three high breeze-block walls so we weren't in any danger. As we grew, we got more privileges until finally we were given most of the front garden to play in addition to this. Access to the front garden is controlled by an additional cat flap.

I have to describe the layout of our roaming area in order to put the next part of the story into context: The perimeter of our front garden is bounded by a mix of lattice and wooden trellis with a special flexible mesh on top so we can't get onto the road – unless someone accidently leaves the gate wide open and what were the chances of that happening? (A few years later I found out – but that is an entirely separate adventure story for another day.)

Three sides of our safe little yard is constructed of high breeze block walls, but on one side it consisted of a series of six foot tall wooden lattice panels which were bolted together to keep us safe. This trellis section of the back yard boundary incorporated a tall external door with a cat flap at the bottom that gives my sister and I access to the front garden. We regularly used the cat flap when we wanted to play in the front garden as opposed to the confines of our back yard.

The day started much like any other when my sister and I ventured out, passing through the kitchen door into the backyard, through the external cat flap for a patrol around our front garden. We spent about twenty minutes there sniffing and checking our territory. After a good mooch it was time to go back inside.

My sister, who is bolder than I, went back to the house and a few minutes later, I decided to follow her. What I *hadn't* noticed however, was that since our trip into the front garden, a human being had arrived and started sawing and doing wood work in our backyard. His name was "Ken the Joiner." Now Ken does like cats and it's a lucky thing he does because that day he had to rescue me.

He'd carelessly placed his tool box right in front of my cat flap, obscuring the entrance. I couldn't get back indoors. Realising I would have to confront this stranger to get back inside where my food was, and believing there was no other way around my dilemma, I foolishly tried to squeeze my ample body *under* the trellis. At the base of the trellis was a layer of small pebbly gravel. Fortunately for me, this is a 'forgiving surface'. I shoved my head between the trellis and the gravel, got as far as my shoulders and kept on pushing. I was *determined!* I have no explanation for what happened next, but here's Ken to tell you:

"Pie started to struggle. He'd pushed so far and then got stuck around his girth. So then he rotated himself so that his tummy was uppermost, and in a blind panic he started thrashing around with his chubby legs and got himself even more stuck!"

Oh dear. The shame!

I was well and truly wedged right across my tummy as I lay on my back, wildly kicking my legs. But Ken's swift actions saved the day. He grabbed both of my hind legs and forced the trellis upwards by a millimetre or two, or as much as it would permit. He had to pull quickly as I was panic-stricken. With a sudden WHOOSH I was suddenly free again. Not waiting to thank my rescuer, I rushed inside, hoping he wouldn't tell anyone.

How wrong I was.

When I took part in #PetFitClub—the UK National competition where selected finalist pets compete to lose weight over a period of six months—they used the fact that I'd got myself stuck under a fence mercilessly and relentlessly! Everyone couldn't believe it could happen to a cat. It can't ever happen again as the layout has now been changed.

I'm over the embarrassment now. I've gotten used to it, but what I won't forgive Ken for is his statement to my folks when he related the story: "I've just had to rescue your cat today, you know – the one *expecting kittens!*"

Pie's story is donated by Brenda Sandland @Mr_Pie

THE FARM BOSS

I'm a sixteen-year-old Tabby named Thomas, but my friends call me Tom.

I came to live with my new family when my owner died while waiting for a heart transplant. I was very worried about who would take care of me, but one day as I was napping in my favorite rocking chair, a man and lady came to visit. Turns out the man was my owner's cousin, and the lady was his wife. I put on my saddest face, and as the lady pet me, she said that I could come to live with them on their farm after they had supervised the auction sale of my home.

Six weeks later I was on my way to my new home. It was about a three hour journey, but I got to stop at the accountant's office who was my new Mom's cousin and another cat lover. There I was given the royal treatment: fresh water, treats and lots of pets. I felt like a celebrity, as not too many cats get to deliver estate books.

When I got to my new home, a farm, I was afraid at first, especially when I met Pokey, a German Shepherd. But then I met my human Sisfur who cuddled me the whole first day, and I knew everything would be okay.

I soon became accustomed to my new surroundings and patrolled everywhere. There was so much to do. I had to oversee the farming operation including repairing machinery, loading grain, or just sitting and waiting for Dad to come home from the field.

There was also Mom's garden and flowers to tend to, and I became good at that. I did twirls in the laneway, and even though Mom worried about this, every one stopped for me. After all, I had sat on a fence post at my old home along the highway, and counted traffic. I loved to jump to the top of the cupboards and hide behind Mom's collector plates, or sit on the roof of the house where I could see everything.

I loved being 'The Farm Boss.' Life was great!

One day I tried to pee, but I couldn't. The pain was excruciating! I hid in the closet, hoping it would go away. When Mom came home from work, I didn't greet her as usual. She called me, but I was in too much pain to care. Mom found me, cuddled me and offered me tuna. When I wouldn't even look at tuna, she knew I was very sick. She wrapped me in a blanket, and she and Dad rushed me to emergency, about an hour away.

The kind vet said I had a blocked bladder and needed immediate surgery. I didn't know what that meant, but I knew my peeps were very worried. I wasn't worried because I knew Dr. Bibby would take good care of me. I didn't like that I had to have some of my fur shaved, but everything went well and I got to go home after two days.

Things were good. Mom and Dad were so happy to see me, and my Sisfur was home for a holiday. Everything was fine until I tried to pee. The pain was terrible and I was passing blood. I was again rushed to see Dr. Bibby, who was concerned. I heard him telling my family the kindest thing to do would be to put me to sleep. They didn't know I could hear, but I could. I also saw Mom and Sisfur crying. Then Mom signed a paper.

Me go OTRB? No way! I wasn't ready, plus I didn't want my staff to be sad. So I made up my mind to get better and go home.

Dr. Bibby, a very compassionate man, said he wouldn't do 'anything' to me until morning, and that he would observe me all through the night. Thank goodness, because I showed signs of feeling better by the next day.

And the next day, and the next! In three days I was on my way home.

I went back to supervising the farm, sleeping with Pokey, and keeping my staff on their toes. And of course, demanding lots of treats. Mom said I was more spoiled than ever.

One day, about six years ago, my friend Pokey went OTRB. I missed him so much, but realized it was up to me to take on his jobs, so I became the farm watchdog/watchcat. I sat on the hill and listened for vehicles to come down the road and up the lane. I knew the sound of each staff's car or truck, and went to meet them. I took over Pokey's job as farm greeter.

Four years ago the peeps got the crazy idea to sell the farm. I didn't want to move, but Dad said it was time. I really worried when I saw all the boxes being packed. Boxes are to sleep in or play in, but not to be packed full of stuff. Was I going to have to find a new home with new peeps?

One day we moved all the boxes—and me—to a new house on a very busy corner in town. I had always been an indoor/outdoor cat, but now Mom wouldn't let me go outside because she feared I would get run over as the cars here wouldn't always stop for kitties like they did on the farm.

I liked my new home from the start. My staff was the same, and they provided compensation for me being an indoor kitty by giving me an attached, heated garage where I could do twirls in the dust under the cars. I also had a big window where I could watch Bird TV.

Then, about three years ago, Mom noticed that I was drinking more water, and using the litter box more frequently. She worried that I had diabetes, so off we went to see Dr. Bibby who confirmed she was right. He told her she had two choices: Insulin shots, or—

(I covered my ears so I couldn't hear).

Well, of course Mom said, "Show me how to give him the shots."

From then on I got poked once a morning for a while, but now I get 5cc's of insulin morning and night. Because Dr. Bibby said I have to eat with the shots, I use this as an excuse to demand tuna or other special treats. Mom always gives in.

One night Mom was away and left Dad in charge. The shot went well, and I was fine when Mom came home. I got cuddles and went out to the garage where I liked to sleep. But during the night I didn't feel well. When morning came I could hear Dad calling, "Tom! Tom!" but I couldn't move. Mom found me lying under her jeep. She thought I had gone OTRB. I knew I had to do something to show her I was still alive, so I managed to move one paw.

When Dad said, "I hope I didn't give him too much insulin," Mom realized I was in a diabetic coma and shouted for Dad to get the glucose spray. She forced my mouth open and shot the spray down my throat. I soon felt better, and when I opened my eyes I saw Mom was crying—again. *She sure spends a lot of time crying over nothing,* I thought. *I'm going to be fine.*

Mom called Dr. Bibby who told her to give me liquid honey. I would be good. Dad, however, didn't feel so good. He felt terrible. Mom told me it was a good thing I had revived because if I hadn't, Dad might have had another heart attack due to his worry.

I got lots of cuddles and treats that day, and my hoomin Sisfurs came to see me. Turns out the syringe Dad had used to give me my insulin was different than the one Mom used, thus causing my little episode. Since that happened, I have never had another diabetic reaction.

Last fall Dr. Bibby said I needed my teeth cleaned. I told Mom I didn't think that was necessary, but she took me to my dental appointment anyway. The cleaning wasn't too bad, but my blood work showed that my kidneys were starting to fail. Dr. Bibby prescribed Asodyl twice a day, so now I not only get two shots, but pills too.

I hate pills, and will do anything to not have to take them, but my staff is relentless, and will not be deterred—even if I have to scratch and draw blood to prove it. Now Mom wraps me in a towel, and holds me while Dad uses a pill pusher to shoot the nasty Asodyl down my throat.

Funny though, my Sisfurs can pill me without a big To-Do when they are cat sitting. I guess that's because they are as stubborn as I am, so I know I might as well give in and take the pill. Mom says I am very fortunate that both my Sisfurs live nearby and look after me when Mom and Dad are away. They really are pawsome sitters.

I know I am much loved by all my peeps—even my ninety-three-year-old Grandma. She always says she would like to hold me, but is afraid I might scratch her. I would never deliberately scratch her, but there is a rumor going around that someone—a nephew—used to call me 'Scratchy' when he was little.

So that's my story. These days I still listen for my staff to drive into the garage so I can meet them at the door. I love to sit in the open window and sniff the fresh air. And I like to sit on the rug at Dad's feet when he's reading or watching TV because I enjoy getting lots of foot pets. I also still follow Mom around when she does her chores, or sit on her lap if she's watching TV.

I may not be a Farm Boss anymore, but I'm still 'Boss Cat' in this household.

Tom's story is donated by Verna Gibb @GibbVerna

LUCKY ~ THE PUPPYCAT

Hi, I'm Lucky the Puppycat. How did I get my name, you ask? Well, twelve short years ago on a beautiful sunny day in February, I was wandering the parking lot of a patrol station, dirty and starving, when I spotted the human I was going to pick for my mom. I walked right up to her and gave her my warmest mew, a loving leg rub, and shined my big blue eyes right at her. She was hooked. She took me home where I met my other mommy, who helped feed and bathe me. They first thought I was a brown kitty from all the dirt in my fur, but after my bath they discovered I was blonde. In fact, the vet confirmed that I was a Creampoint Siamese, malnourished, but otherwise healthy. They found me quite irresistible and had no choice but to let me stay. I was lucky to find a home with wonderful humans.

What's that? You want to know about why I'm called a Puppycat? Actually, not many people understand what a Puppycat is. A Puppycat is a cat that has the best behavioral qualities of a dog. It's the best of both worlds really: the love and loyalty of a dog, paired with the independence and self-maintenance of a cat. Mommy says there is such thing as a kittydog as well, which is the opposite: A dog with some of the cute behavioral qualities of a cat.

But I digress. You are obviously more interested in what makes me a Puppycat. I don't blame you.

As I started to get acquainted with my new forever home, I wanted Mommy to discover my Puppycat qualities and have her fall deeply in love with me. First, I showed her how I can play fetch. She gave me a pink mouse toy that I named Pinkmousey. She would throw Pinkmousey anywhere in the house and I would go running, pick him up in my mouth, trot back to Mommy, and drop him at her feet for another throw.

Puppycat quality #1: Fetch. Check!

Next I showed her how I always wanted to be near her. I would follow Mommy around the house. Up the stairs, into the bathroom, on the bed, on the couch, at the dinner table, in the study, in the weight room... Wherever she went, I would follow. Once she would settle in a room, I would go fetch my favorite toy, drop it near, and nestle down with her.

Puppycat quality #2: Attachment. Check!

Now my favorite time is spending quality time on the couch with my moms. I usually snuggle up to Mommy, always having to touch her in some way. I like to lay between her legs, draping over her leg or foot, or lay on her tummy and cuddle her arm. If I am next to her, I will reach out and put my paw on her arm just so I can feel her near. But my favorite position is to lay my head on her hand. I fall fast asleep. I call this a 'hand pillow' and invented the #handpillowcaturday hashtag on Twitter for all my kitty friends to see my photos with Mommy and share their own.

Puppycat quality #3: Lapdog. Check!

Did I mention that Pinkmousey is my favorite toy? Actually, he is more like my one and only toy. He is older than I am at 15+ years and the only toy I enjoy playing with. I like to carry him around the house and bring him to whatever room Mommy is settled in. I also like to sit at the top of the stairs with Pinkmousey in my mouth and sing a howling, loud lullaby. Mommy loves that right at bedtime.

I remember the one time I lost Pinkmousey. I sulked around the house for days trying to find him. Mom tried to give me a new Pinkmousey, but it didn't fool me. That one was an imposter and I knew it. My moms even helped me look all over the house for him, but we couldn't find him. I was so sad. Mom finally found Pinkmousey in her work boot in the closet when she was getting ready for work three days later. I couldn't have been more happy to have my one and only favorite toy back that day. Now, he never leaves my sight.

Puppycat quality #4: Commitment. Check!

I am very trainable too. Mommy trained me to walk on a leash, although I don't go for walks. And she trained me to stay on the porch when we are outside. But most of all, I learned voice commands. I know "Out please" to leave a room. "Inside please" to come in from the outside. "Closer please" to bring Pinkmousey closer to Mommy's reach when playing fetch, and "Up please" to get up on the bathtub ledge so Mommy can apply my ear cream medication. I like polite commands. I also obey, "Come here," and "Time for bed." As for "Get off the table..." Well, I am a cat, after all. Still working on that one.

Puppycat quality #5: Semi-Obedience. Check!

Who doesn't like a belly rub? Oh yeah, that's a majority of cats. You may be able to get one or two rubs in, but then the ATTACK comes. This is because cats usually trust no one. Me? I love belly rubs! I will lie on my back next to Mommy, expose my belly and invite the belly rub. I let her rub my belly for hours. I trust that she will keep me safe and treat me well. I enjoy it so much that I can fall asleep with her rubbing my belly.

Puppycat quality #6: Trusting. Check!

Lastly, the most doggie-like behavior that I have is my outward expression of love and devotion. If Mommy talks to me, I talk back. When I hear Mommy coming home from work, I run over to my white tiger stool in front of the back door and wait for her to come in so she can pet me first thing. I get excited to follow her to her next destination in the house. I wag my tail when she is rubbing my belly or petting my head and back. I rub my head on her hand and hug her arm when we cuddle on the couch. I will give Mommy kisses and she doesn't even have to have food. I will lay with her in bed when she is not feeling well and purr her to better health. I love my Mommy and I show it to her in every way I can.

Puppycat quality #7: Adoration. Check!

So now that you know what a Puppycat is, you can understand how you can fall in love with one. We are great for training doggie lovers to love cats because we have the qualities and behaviors they are used to experiencing with a fur baby. Not that my moms were strictly doggie lovers, but they did have many doggie lover friends who, after meeting me, said if they ever got a kitty, it would have to be just like me. Puppycats are just cool like that.

I am happy that I found my moms and had the opportunity to show them how loving and devoted I am. And my moms feel extra lucky for having been adopted by such a wonderful Puppycat like me. Their Lucky charm the Puppycat. Yes, that's me.

Lucky's story is donated by Michelle Rueda @LuckyDaPuppycat

HELEN
THE DEAF AND BLIND RACCOON

Since 2007 my yard has been used by raccoons to raise their families. I provide water pools, dog food and peanuts, and in return they drive away poisonous snakes.

When I step outside with kibble, they gather around my feet to escort me down the slope to where my yard skirts a tree-lined creek. Throughout the summer into fall, the babies learn to trust me, and by early winter when they are old enough to be on their own, they continue to return. And, as Mother Nature intends, they bring their babies to my yard the following spring.

The cycle continues.

I met Helen the summer of 2011. When I approached, her siblings ran for the woods, but she did not. I soon realized she was both blind and deaf. I could slide food right under her nose, but she had no idea I was there. Her nose, however, was in perfect working order. She loved peanut butter sandwiches. I often saw her eating by the pool...alone. The size of a basketball, she would have been easy pickings for a stray dog or a fox to kill her. I had to do something.

When I called Petra at the wildlife rehabilitation center, I barely got the words 'blind and deaf baby' out of my mouth when she asked, "Do you have her trapped?"

Well...no. I have enough cats to know what goes into their mouths comes out their bottoms. I was not going to catch Helen until I knew I could hand her off *immediately*.

A live trap would not work as I would catch every member of Helen's family before she stumbled into the trap. Petra advised me to put a blanket over Helen, sweep her up and put her into a box, then call her. Uh…too simple.

Which meant I had to put my own sweet spin on catching her.

I didn't like the idea of throwing a blanket over Helen. I have never caught an animal that way. I prefer luring into a baited trap or cage, and slapping the door shut. It worked several times on the wildest of feral cats, so that was the route I decided to take.

I found a large box, a blanket, gloves (I'm no fool—seriously), and was making two peanut butter sandwiches when my husband called. I told him what I'd planned for the day. He made a scoffing sound. "What?" I demanded.

"It's not going to be as simple as you make it sound," he said. "It's never simple with you. There's always a bigger story."

We agreed to disagree and hung up, with Ray saying he couldn't wait to hear the bigger story, and me sticking my tongue out at my cell phone.

It didn't take long before I spied Helen lunching with her family. I waited until the others returned to the woods, then grabbed the box, gloves and sandwiches, along with the lid from a plastic storage bin. I walked up to Helen and set the box on end so she would walk into it. I also said a prayer that I would be smart about trapping her. I didn't want to frighten her. Imagine being deaf and blind, and suddenly something grabs you!

Meanwhile Helen sat in the middle of the kibble, munching happily. She always had a perpetually happy smile on her face. I hated to upset her.

I baited the box with one sandwich, then tore off a corner of the other and slipped it under her nose. She went right for it. I gave her a really small portion, but it took her like, ten minutes to eat it. Meanwhile I'm standing over her, baking in the sun, itchy from the flies buzzing around the damp kibble.

When she finished, she picked up another piece of kibble. My patience was wearing thin. I was ready for both Helen and I to get on with our lives. But then she smelled more peanut butter and headed for the box. Yay! Except she stopped to sniff the strange object. And then she backed away. Darn. But then she walked in part way. Ahhh, the power of peanut butter.

While she was eating her sandwich, I used the storage bin lid to nudge her forward, while tipping the box up on end. Helen tumbled into the bottom and before she could make a sound, I had the lid taped shut. Yep. I taped it shut using two strips of tape designed for sealing storage boxes. It had to be good tape. My husband doesn't buy cheap stuff.

I called Petra who cheered, and we made plans to meet half way. I then secured Helen in the backseat of my car and off we went. She rode quietly for ten minutes. I could hear her eating her sandwich. Then...she finished.

Ruh roh!

The box in the back seat with the happy, smiling, deaf and blind baby raccoon began to rustle. I had one eye on the road and one eye on the box...not easy to do. I was thankfully on a backwoods highway with nary a car in sight. *Very* thankful when I turned around for a third time and saw Helen sticking her nose out of the box top.

Looked like Ray's theory that I always had a bigger story was about to come true...which pissed me off! Yeah, I had taped the box shut. Two whole pieces! Dirty rotten cheap tape. Ray's tape! At least I had something to blame on him.

I pulled off the highway and shook the box, thinking Helen would huddle quietly in the bottom for the rest of the drive. Nope. She ramped it up. Deaf and blind—yes. Raccoon with claws—damn skippy!

I finally flipped the box upside down, with the top against the seat, hoping Helen would quietly sit on it and I could drive and...

Nope! She dug her claws into the bottom that was now the top, reminding me of the time I thought I had a feral cat secured in a cat carrier on the seat next to me while driving to the vet...except he kept head-butting the door and actually *punched it out* so that he crawled out of the carrier...while I'm driving...one eye on the road, the other eye on the feral now head-butting my windshield less than two feet away.

Envisioning a reenactment, I threw my purse on top of Helen's box, and held it down with one hand while driving at a slightly accelerated speed. As the box rocked and rolled, I tapped on it, hoping to...not scare her but...communicate. Yes! My tapping was me spelling w-a-t-e-r to Helen, reassuring her she didn't need to panic cuz I was doing enough of that for both of us.

I prayed my exit was coming up next. It was! I then prayed Petra would be pulling into the gas station parking lot at the same time I was...and she did. *Thank you, Jesus!*

Petra got out of her van with paperwork. Clearly she thought I had everything under control and we could do a little business before making the transfer. I guess my wild eyes and shriek about Helen wanting out of the box *NOW* made Petra toss aside her paperwork to open the car door.

As Helen's arm reached out from the hole she had chewed, Petra calmly pushed the paw back inside. She then dropped a towel into the box and scooped up *my* raccoon. Helen hung limp in her hands like a rag doll...not anything like the boxed maniac terrorizing me down I-69. "She has no eyes," Petra finally said. "There is nothing there."

Aw. I felt bad for thinking of Helen as a maniac. She didn't have eyes!

Petra determined Helen was three months old, and was amazed she had lived that long. I wasn't. With two kid pools and food delivery twice a day, Helen didn't have to go far from her bed to get food and water. We have quiet neighbors. No dogs. No children. Ideal in every way to nurture a baby raccoon with birth defects.

I was teary driving home, relieved Helen would have the care she needed. Relieved there are Petra's in this world devoted to animals in desperate need. Relieved I wouldn't have to worry about the helpless little basketball of fluff groping her way around my yard.

Five years later, I think of Helen often. Her brother, Huck, who is blind in one eye, greets me at the back door every morning to escort me down the slope to where my yard skirts a tree-lined creek. I worried about him being an outcast for a couple of years until he met Becky, and they had babies. Several litters in fact.

The cycle continues.

Helen's story is donated by author Kimberley Koz.
www.KimberleyKoz.com / www.Wonderpurr.com.
@KimberleyKoz

MARIO DA CAT

In September 2008 my husband, Don, and I returned home to an empty house from a trip to Italy with our daughter and her husband for our 50th Anniversary. We dearly missed our cat, Misty, who had to be euthanized due to severe kidney failure. My husband, who had grown up with dogs, said to me, "If one would like to adopt another cat, how does one go about it?"

I will never forget his statement as Misty was the third cat we had adopted. We had only been home a couple of hours from our trip, and he already missed having an animal to greet us. I did too, so I told him, "Tomorrow we can make a trip to the Humane Society and see who needs to be adopted."

The next morning, a Saturday, we visited the Humane Society. They had a large room where they socialized kitties. I recall there were about eight cats in there at the time. A female calico caught my eye. She was beautiful. During the 50 years we had been married, we had enjoyed three cats: one black and white, and two grey tabbies. We loved all of them dearly, but... that calico female at the shelter really caught my eye!

Don and I walked through the doors into the cat room and were immediately greeted by a black and white kitty who did everything he could do to make my husband notice him. First he head-butted Don, then he wound himself around Don's legs, and then stretched himself up Don's legs, along with all the other endearing things kitties do to get noticed.

As I walked over to see the Calico (who ignored me), Don said, "Why don't we adopt this one?" Of course he was referring to the black and white kitty that was turning himself inside out trying to get noticed. Don picked him up and the kitty filled the room with loud purrs. Meanwhile, I continued to try to make friends with Miss Snooty, who continued to ignore me.

Again Don said, while sitting with the black and white cat on his lap, "Why don't we take this one?"

I recommended we go home and think about it. Not rush into anything. Secretly I held out hope for the aloof Calico to pay attention to me. That day we returned home without a kitty. I realize now I was being a pain in the neck, but I just had it in my head that I wanted a pretty color instead of black, white or grey. Nasty of me, wasn't it?

The next day, Sunday, we returned to the shelter and had the identical experience as the day before. The black and white kitty did everything he could do to tell us he wanted to go home with us, while the Calico remained aloof. Again I suggested we wait another day. I was so certain Miss Snooty would eventually come around.

She didn't.

On Monday I called our vet to see if she could do a physical that day before we brought the black and white kitty home. Overnight I'd come to terms with Miss Snooty's rejection and realized the black and white cat had to be ours. After all, he had made it purrrfectly clear that he wanted us to be his humans.

Without telling Don, I went back to the Shelter and adopted the black and white kitty: Mario. I stopped at the vet's clinic on the way home, and he was pronounced in good health—except he needed to have his teeth cleaned and maybe a tooth or two pulled at some point. Needless to say, Don was very happy when I showed up at home with Mario.

We immediately took Mario to our basement to show him where the litter box was and to let him explore the area with attached family room and office. As Don sat in his recliner, Mario jumped into his lap and started purring. Then he settled down and took a nap. At last he had his very own Forever Home. He didn't even care to see the other part of the house. He was simply happy to be home!

When it was bed time, Mario still didn't want to explore the main level of the house. Instead he joined us in our bedroom, promptly hopped up on the bed and snuggled between us.

Mario was adopted in October 2008 at approximately 2.6 years of age. He had been living at the Humane Society for 4 months after being turned in by a lady who found him wandering the streets. We were told he was in pretty rough shape when turned in. Don and I both feel he had a good home at one point because he is a real people kitty and loves attention.

In December 2009 our regular vet pulled 3 teeth and cleaned the others. Infection set in and a course of four different antibiotics were tried. None seemed to work. When I took him back for a check-up, our vet told me, "I think Mario might be one of those rare kitties who are allergic to his own tooth decay. I recommend you see an Animal Dentist." I didn't even know there was such a thing as an animal dentist!

The only animal dentist in our state had two offices with the closest being 60 miles from our city. At the end of July 2009, Mario saw the dentist in Oshkosh, Wisconsin where he was diagnosed with Gingivostomatitis. The dentist required $2,500 for the consultation, which covered putting Mario under anesthesia, extensive x-rays, blood work, etc.

This was a large chunk of change for my husband and I, as we are both retired and living on a fixed income. We had already spent $1,618 at our regular vet since adopting Mario nine months prior, but Mario was worth it. So—with a huge gulp!—we agreed to go ahead with the surgery. The dentist could not tell us what our total bill would be because it depended on what he found after all the x-rays and thorough exam. The news was not good. Mario had Stomatitis. Dr. Kessler recommended pulling all of Mario's teeth, but indicated he would try to save the canine teeth if we promised to brush those four teeth twice daily, which we did.

To make a long story short, Mario had to have all of his teeth removed surgically, as he had an advanced case of Stomatitis. By December 2009 Mario was toothless and we were another $4,400+ poorer. With the hope we wouldn't run short before our final days on earth, we took the money out of our retirement savings. As Mario had already found a permanent place in our hearts, we felt he was worth the huge investment.

I am excited about FourPawsLifeline.org. I see it as an excellent resource for many people who simply don't have any funds to draw upon for rising vet bills. We never know when a major emergency will pop up for our beloved fur babies. How sad it would have been for us to have to deny Mario a chance to live the healthy life he has been leading since November 2009 after having all his teeth pulled. We had the money and were able to pay for it, but so many people cannot come up with funds.

Mario's story is donated by Mary Roever. @MarioDaCat

A WONDERPURR LIFE

Herman closed the book. "This is a Wonderpurr collection of tales," he murmured to himself. "It will surely help to bring attention and donations to Four Paws Lifeline."

"Are there no more stories?" Dori asked.

Herman startled. He had been so absorbed in the amazing tales written about his Anipal friends, he had forgotten he was reading the book as a bedtime story to his sister.

"No more stories. The book is done. Time for bed."

Dori clutched her blanket. "But, where is your story?"

Herman blinked. "My story?"

"Many of our Anipal friends have their story in the book. Where is your story?"

Herman shrugged. "I'm getting older. I don't remember much about my early years."

Dori's eyes watered. "But... I was a good girl today. I didn't break anything. I want to hear about when you were little like me."

Herman's whiskers twitched with humor. "I don't remember back that far."

"But I do." Herman and Dori turned to see their Mom standing in the doorway. "Your Dad and I lived on five acres in Kentucky. Our house was at the top of a steep hill, surrounded by thick woods.

You arrived during a blizzard."

Dori looked at her brother with amazement. "Just like Frosty the Snowman!" She scooted over so Herman could craw into bed beside her, and together hear his story.

"You were about eight months old when I found you in my front yard," Mom continued as she sat beside them. "You must have been lost for a long time because you were covered with tree sap that had hardened your fur into something that resembled a turtle's shell. I tried to cut it off, but it was too thick, so I took you to the veterinarian to shave it off. When I returned to take you home, I put you in a blue doggy sweater to keep you warm because you had no fur."

Dori giggled behind her paw. "You were nekked, Hwermie."

"We had older cats, but hadn't had a kitten in years, so we weren't prepared for how much energy Herman had. He didn't walk. He bounced like Tigger from Winnie the Pooh. He loved to zoom down the stairs, through the kitchen, through the living room, and back up the stairs. I fed Herman beside our oldest, Buddy, a diabetic tabby who lived to be 22 years old, so Herm could learn manners. He used to smack his lips when he ate. Well, one day while he was hunkered over his dish making quite a noise, Buddy bopped him on the back of his head, mushing his face down into his food."

While Dori giggled, Herman said, "I should do that to you."

"You had great enthusiasm," Mom continued. "Everything was Wonderpurr and new, and needed to be fully explored. You started each day as though someone had just pushed your ON button. From a dead sleep you would leap to your feet and with twitters, chirps, and screams—you've never had a typical cat's meow—you would race from your bed to start your day.

"I remember one day—vividly—when I had just opened a hot oven and saw a flash of white from the corner of my eye. Without thinking I grabbed it. You! You almost jumped into a hot oven!"

Dori looked at Herman with huge eyes. "Even I never did that."

"Another time I found you inside the dryer with the door closed. And when I opened a cupboard I found you inside riding the Lazy Susan. Still another time I stopped you from eating a live wasp."

"You were a handful," Dori told him.

"Did I break stuff?" Herman asked his mom. His ears had turned pink with embarrassment.

"No, I don't recall you ever breaking anything." She turned

with Herman to look pointedly at Dori, who hung her head. "But you won first place in the PetsMart Halloween costume contest. You went dressed as a Guardian Angel to Firemen, wearing angel wings and a fireman's hat. You also helped me raise a baby robin that fell from its nest down the chimney. Bob the robin took a liking to you, and would perch on the side of your bowl and eat alongside you. You were a very good birdie babysitter. Bob the Robin is the title of our next book, due out later this year."

"Tell me more about Herman getting in trouble," Dori pleaded.

"He didn't get in trouble often, however..." Mom looked at Herman. "Do you recall the woods that surrounded our home in Kentucky?"

Herman shrugged, and pretended he had an itch.

"Like I said, Herman loved to zoom. And occasionally he would zoom right past our feet when the door opened. That was a risk because we lived in the middle of very thick woods where deer, fox, wild dogs and coyotes also lived. Herman would race from the porch and head straight for the woods. Of course I was usually wearing my pink bunny slippers, but after the second time he ran past me, I made sure to have a pair of slip-on shoes ready to chase after him. On two occasions I remember being very afraid I wouldn't find him. But, of course, I did."

Mom rubbed Herman's head. "You always came to me when you heard my voice. And you still do. Years later when you decided to travel with me to Blogpaws, I remember I left you in the hotel room to nap while I went to lunch. But when I stepped out of the elevator onto our floor, I heard you yelling through the door, all the way down the hall and around the corner. You have impressive lungs, little man."

"There was nothing on TV," Herman told her. "I was bored."

"You surprised me at Blogpaws. I didn't know you would turn into such a rock star. We've never had dogs, and yet you were very chill with all the dogs who came over to meet you. I remember pushing you in your open stroller through the hotel lobby when a Great Dane walked past and stuck his head into the stroller to lick you. I was horrified that he could have bitten you."

"I was horrified, too," Herman said. "I stunk like doggy spit."

"You walked on a leash for the first time in Vegas. You were a little constipated from your first airplane ride so we took you out on the hotel grounds to walk, never expecting you would lead us all over the garden and then right up the sidewalk into the hotel and through the lobby. But that was small compared to you walking the red carpet for the Nose to Nose award banquet. You walked the carpet in Vegas and again in Nashville. I am so very proud of you."

Dori nuzzled his cheek. "Me too. I cry in the car when Mom takes me for my yearly vaccinations."

"You make me proud when you accompany me to book signings to promote our children's story, *Finding Mya*. And now you will be promoting your new purranormal mystery series, Sherlock Herms..."

"With me as your co-star," Dori chimed in.

"But, I was especially proud when you traveled to Chattanooga to help @DylCat1's mom, Sara, feel better because she missed Dylan while being in the hospital for so long. You could have been a therapy cat. You always make people happy, just by being you. But I'm glad you decided on a career as my writer's muse. You're the best inspurration I've ever had."

As she kissed his bowed head, Herman's purr filled the room.

"Thank you for helping me edit this book," Mom said, picking up *Four Paws and 31 Tales*. "By launching Four Paws Lifeline, Belle's parents are providing a much needed service to people who cannot afford emergency veterinary care."

Dori bumped his shoulder. "Hwermie the Edipurr."

"And now, both of you into bed." Mom drew the blanket over them, and kissed their brows. "Sweet dreams." She turned off the light and closed the door.

As a sweet honeysuckle breeze flowed through the open window, they lay silently for a time, listening to the sound of crickets and cicadas in the yard.

"I'm really proud of you," Dori murmured. "You never broke anything."

Herman nuzzled her brow. "I'm sure that's not true. Mom has a short memory. Plus she likes to remember just the good stuff. She will forget you break things when you're my age."

Realizing his little sister had fallen asleep, Herman lay for a while, thinking about the stories he had read tonight. So many of his Anipal friends had suffered before they found their Forever Homes. He had been lucky to find his home without enduring anything more than having his fur covered with hardened tree sap.

He also knew he was fortunate to live with people who were able to afford the many vet bills that came with pets as they aged. He recalled his two older brothers, Nicholas and Cookie, who died the same year from respiratory disease brought on by black mold in the air handlers. Mom had spent thousands of dollars trying to find out why they were sick, and then more money trying to make them well. They had been too weak to live, but because their veterinarian, Brandy Ellis, figured out they had mold in the house, Nick and Cookie hadn't died in vain. They were heroes. They sacrificed their lives so everyone else could live.

That's why Four Paws Lifeline was so important. They could help with the cost of emergency or critical care for pet parents who didn't have the money. All the stories in *Four Paws and 31 Tales* were donated by pet-loving parents, and the profits from the book went directly into Four Paws Lifeline's non-profit fund to benefit the sick animals.

As Herman drifted off to sleep, he said a prayer for all the homeless animals on the streets, and for the abused and neglected.

Prayer for the Animals
by Albert Schweitzer

Hear our humble prayer, O God, for our friends, the animals.
Especially for animals who are suffering; for any that are
hunted or lost or deserted or frightened or hungry;
for all that must be put to death.
We entreat for them all Thy mercy and pity,
and for those who deal with them, we ask a
a heart of compassion and gentle hands and kindly words.
Make us, ourselves, to be true friends to animals,
and so to share the blessings of the merciful.

Herman's story is donated by author Kimberley Koz, mom to Herman @TattleCat and Dori @Adorapurr on Twitter. Herman and Dori's adventures with the Wonderpurr Gang are featured on Kim's website: www.KimberleyKoz.com / www.Wonderpurr.com.

ABOUT FOUR PAWS LIFELINE

Four Paws Lifeline is a 501 (c)(3) non-profit organization.

Our goal is to provide financial assistance to those pet owners who are not able to afford critical care or emergency veterinary care for their furry loved ones.

We are here to offer hope in your pet's darkest hour. We feel that their life should not depend on your ability to pay. Rushing a beloved pet to the emergency vet is stressful and full of fear. To delay treatment because of an inability to afford the treatment only prolongs the pet's suffering. Often animals are surrendered or euthanized as a result of not being able to afford treatment.

We are working towards a future where decisions about companion animal medical care need never be made on the basis of cost. Four Paws Lifeline was started to assistant and to take the worry about money out of the equation.

Four Paws Lifeline relies solely on the support and contributions of individuals who love animals. We need your help to extend hope to those with no voice. I know there are many animal lovers out there that have found themselves on the other side of that exam table. Any amount you can donate is appreciated. All donations are tax deductible.

Please visit **www.FourPawsLifeline.org** to learn more about our organization and to lend your financial support to those in need.

Thank you,

Karen and David Brothers
Co-Founders, Four Paws Lifeline

www.FourPawsLifeline.org
A 501(c)(3) non-profit organization
Tax ID #47-2991797
#217
8825 34th Ave NE, Suite L
Tulalip, WA 98271-8086
guardian@FourPawsLifeline.org

97281363R00064

Made in the USA
San Bernardino, CA
22 November 2018